Reaching, Teaching & Pastoring Children

Church of God Children's Ministry Certification Manual

ISBN 978-1-59684-843-6
Editor: Lance Colkmire

Reaching, Teaching, and Pastoring Children
©2015 Pathway Press (revision of the 2007 edition)
Published by Pathway Press, Cleveland, TN, USA

Unless otherwise noted, all Scripture quotations are from
The Holy Bible, New International Version,
©1973, 1978, 1984 by International Bible Society.

Scriptures marked CEV are from
The Holy Bible, Contemporary English Version,
©1995, American Bible Society.

Scriptures marked NCV are from the *New Century Version*,
©2005 Thomas Nelson, Inc.

Scriptures marked NLT are from the *Holy Bible, New Living Translation*,
©1996, 2004, 2007 by Tyndale House Foundation

Scripture quotations marked TLB are from *The Living Bible*,
©1971, Tyndale House Publishers.

Scripture quotations marked NKJV are from
The Holy Bible, New King James Version,
©1985 by Thomas Nelson, Inc.

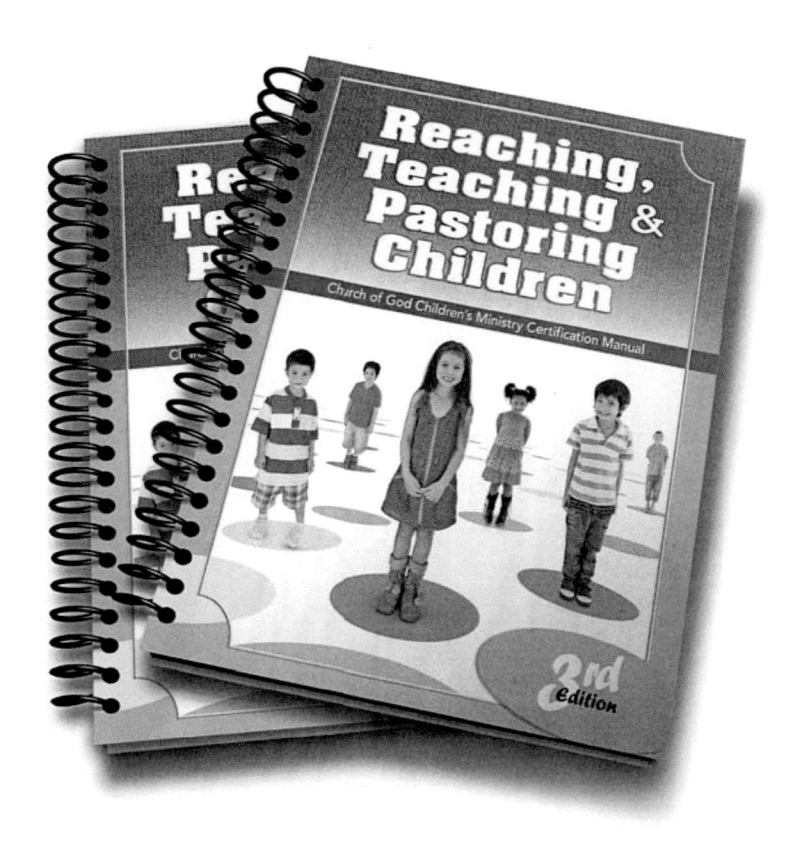

Reaching, Teaching, and Pastoring Children is a product of the Church of God Children's Leaders Association. This manual helps to fulfill the stated purpose of the association:

> To affirm the dignity, credibility and scriptural necessity of ministry to children and to provide those who minister to children a fellowship for the purpose of encouragement, training, and providing resources.

This book provides direction, instruction, and encouragement to those who minister to children. It is especially designed for Pentecostal children's pastors, teachers, and evangelists.

Besides being a ready reference tool, this book also serves as the foundational component of the Children's Ministry Certification Program for the Church of God. Complete information about the program is given at the end of this manual.

Contents

FOUNDATIONS

1. **Help! Where Do I Begin?**
   Cindy Hunnicutt 7

2. **Children in the Church: Covenant Participants**
   Cheryl Bridges Johns 13

ORGANIZATION

3. **Life-Changing Children's Leaders**
   Lance Colkmire & Wilson Kilgore 21

4. **Building a Team: Recruiting, Equipping, and Keeping Volunteers**
   Cindy Hunnicutt 29

5. **Financing Ministry to Children**
   Irma Hendrix 35

CHILDREN

6. **Reaching the "In Between" Preteens**
   Cindy Hunnicutt & Keith Wilson 41

7. **Losing Teeth and Finding God**
   Wanda Brett 49

8. **Loving and Leading Preschoolers**
   Pamela Coker Browning 57

9. **Burps, Diapers, and Joy: Baby Ministry**
   Cheryl Bridges Johns 65

TEACHING THE WORD

10. **Building a Lesson Kids Will Love**
    Wilson Kilgore 75

11. **Scripture Memory: It Can Be Done**
    Lynn Miller 81

12. **Discipling the Undisciplined Child**
    Daniel C. Bunce 87

13. **Welcoming the New Kid**
    Steve Burkowske 91

14. **Leading Children to Christ**
    Lance Colkmire 95

15. **Reaching Unchurched Kids**
    Elaine Shreve 105

DISCIPLESHIP

16. **Helping Kids Develop a Devotional Life**
    Lance Colkmire 113

17. **Reaching Out to Grieving Children**
    Chris Knipp 119

18. **Baptism, Communion, and Footwashing**
    Lance Colkmire 123

19. **Children Can Pray, Walk, and Live in the Spirit**
    Lance Colkmire 135

20. **Helping Kids Find, Develop, and Use Their Gifts**
    Lynn Miller 141

21. **Expecting God to Show Up in Our Children's Worship Service**
    Lynn Miller 151

22. **Let the Children Praise Him!**
    Beth Barnes & Lance Colkmire 157

23. **Show and Tell: Object Lessons**
    Shelia Stewart 163

24. **Developing and Delivering Dynamic Children's Messages**
    Lance Colkmire 169

25. **Altering Kids' Lives at the Altar**
    Lance Colkmire 177

CERTIFICATION

Reflect and Respond 185

Children's Ministry Certification Program 195

Help! Where Do I Begin?

Cindy Hunnicutt

Ministering to children is the most exciting and fulfilling call on one's life. The privilege and responsibility of writing God's Word on the pages of a child's heart is beyond compare. Yet the enormous responsibility of modeling Jesus and His vast love to the children He has placed under your care can cause you to cry, "Help! How do I begin?"

It's always best to begin with the expert—and that, of course, is Jesus himself. Let's see how Jesus approached ministry to children.

Jesus Made Time for Kids (Mark 5:21-43)

In this narrative we see Jesus going out of His way to meet the needs of a 12-year-old girl by going directly to her and spending *quality* (I should say!) time with her. We even see Jesus minimizing the distractions so He can focus in on this little girl.

Spending time with kids is the main thing you can do to prove to "your" children their worth and value. *You* are the Word of God to the children who look up to you. *You* are the one they read.

Following are some easy ideas for spending time with the kids in your ministry.

Make Yourself Available. Before and after regular church service times, be available for kids to talk to you. Be approachable. Let them tell you about their day at school, their dog's injury, their grandparent's illness. These are important issues in children's lives, and they need your undivided attention.

Really listen to the kids. Have a genuine conversation. Take the children seriously. Also, keep an eye out for the shy ones who may not directly approach you, but who hang out on the fringes, hoping you will notice them.

Communicate With Parents. Let parents know you are available to talk to their children individually about problems and difficulties. You do not have to be a professional counselor—just be a listener. Listen, then help the child approach God's throne with his or her problem. Kids and parents alike will think you are the best pastor on the planet! All you've done is provide for the child what we all need—someone to listen to us and love us.

Get in on Outings. Go on outings and activities planned in your department whenever possible. Even if you are not the one to plan a particular activity, try to attend at least part of the event. Kids love to be close to you—they love to be noticed by you. They also like to see you play and be part of their fun.

Focus On a Group. If you are responsible for a large number of children, focus in on one segment if possible. You might develop a drama team that you direct. You might have an ongoing discipleship group for kids who are serious about their walk with Jesus. You could take the top couple of grades of your age group responsibility and plan events and ministry in which you are always involved.

For those who minister to large groups, focusing somewhere is very important. Spreading yourself too thin can wreak havoc on your schedule and home life. Focusing on one area allows you to truly make a difference in the lives of the kids in that group, while managing your personal life as well.

Host Kids. Have a group of kids visit your home for a time of fun, fellowship, Bible study, and prayer. There's something about the kids being in your home that helps them more easily see you as a real, approachable person.

However you accomplish it, model yourself after Jesus and make it a priority in your ministry to spend time with kids.

Jesus Was Moved by the Requests of Parents (Matthew 15:21-28; 17:14-18)

In these passages, we read how Jesus cast out demons from two children. In both cases, Jesus acted in response to the faith and persistence of a parent.

We, too, must listen to the requests of parents regarding the needs of their children.

Parents are concerned with the well-being of their children, and it is up to you to respond to those concerns. The parents of the children in your ministry want to make sure their children are being taught the Word of God. For some of those parents, you will be affirming and supporting what is being taught at home. For others, the expectation will be for you to fill in the gaps being created at home. Either way, God has given you a tremendous spiritual responsibility that must not be taken lightly.

Parents are also concerned with the physical well-being of their children. Can they trust you with the physical safety of their child? Are the rooms in the church building free of safety hazards? Are the classrooms under control so parents feel secure leaving their children there? Are outings and special events well-chaperoned and well-planned? Do you return when you say you will? Are permission slips and release forms used? Are behavior guidelines enforced? Take a cue from Jesus and respond to the parents as you endeavor to minister to their children.

Jesus Taught That Kindness to Children Will Be Rewarded (Matthew 10:42)

No part of ministering to children is insignificant. Jesus tells us we will not lose our reward when we demonstrate even the smallest act of kindness to a child.

If taking a child to the restroom is necessary, do it! If chairs need to be straightened, do it! If you need to pray for the healing of a child's paper cut for the third time, do it! Don't overlook the small things. A cup of Kool-aid® given in the name of Jesus pleases the Father, and He will reward you. Show yourself faithful in the small things, pay attention to the details, and you will be building a ministry that will last for the long haul.

Jesus Welcomed Children (18:1-6, 10-14)

We could write an entire chapter of this book regarding this passage of Scripture, but suffice it to say that Jesus told us to welcome children and to in no way cause them to sin.

How do we welcome children? How do we ensure we are not a stumbling block to them?

As a leader you must have a tender, humble heart toward your children. Don't be harsh or demanding, even when the children are exasperating. Choose teachers and helpers under you who adhere to this approach in their dealings with children.

Jesus uses very strong language in this passage regarding those who hinder children. Did He really mean that it would be better for those who cause a child to sin to be "drowned in the depths of the sea" (v. 6)? Evidently He did, or He would not have said it! Make sure your approach with children is that of the shepherd mentioned later on in this passage: willing to risk the ministry he had built (the flock of 99) for the sake of the one (vv. 12-14).

Sometimes we unwittingly cause children to feel unwelcome in our ministry by the way we physically present our ministry to them. Is the children's ministry area dark and dingy? Are you recycling your curriculum for the third time, rather than seeking God for a fresh approach? Stumbling blocks come in many forms, even in seemingly innocuous ways such as room décor and curriculum choices.

Your love of the children God has placed in your care should be seen even in the way you present the gospel to them. Be creative! Use variety in your approaches. Your worst method of presenting the gospel is the one you use all the time!

Look at your classrooms from the eyes of the children, their parents and your visitors. Are your classrooms cluttered, messy and dingy? Schedule a "de-cluttering day," and then add some fresh paint. Remove the obstacles by creating an environment that causes children to be excited to participate. Bright colors, neat classrooms, and up-to-date methods really put out the welcome mat for kids.

Jesus Touched and Blessed Children (19:13-15)

The children to whom you minister need your appropriate, loving touches. Pats on the back, high fives, and "safe" hugs build self-esteem and love in your kids.

It is also important to do as Jesus did by blessing the kids with your words. Encourage them with words such as these: "I am so glad you are here today"; "You are so _____" (fill in the blank: *patient, kind, obedient, creative, awesome, friendly, loving*).

Your words are incredibly powerful. Your children need to hear words of encouragement from you. Florence Litauer, in her book *Silver Boxes: The Gift of Encouragement*, says our words should come out of our mouths like presents wrapped up, ready to give away. What kind of presents are your children receiving from you?

Jesus Gladly Received the Praises of Children (21:14-16)

One of the greatest privileges as ministers to children is to lead them in praise and worship of God. In chapter 21, we even see Jesus defending the children's right to be present in the Temple praising Him! Notice how Jesus used Scripture to defend the children. He said to the Temple leaders, "Have you never read . . . ?" (v. 16).

Think about that in reference to your own church setting. Many times you are called to be the voice of the children to the leadership of your church, especially when it regards the children's ability to focus on Jesus. In those times, you must base your position on Scripture.

Now, to the practical side of praise and worship—there is a large market of children's praise and worship music available in a variety of formats to suit your needs. Investigate what is out there, and then make sure you choose music that is attractive to kids and geared to their age level as you help them "enter His gates with thanksgiving and his courts with praise" (Ps. 100:4).

In designing a praise and worship service for children, remember these two simple principles:

Praise music tells *about God*—His goodness, what He's done, reminders of who He is. Praise music for kids should be lively and fun to help with another of the purposes of singing with kids: to get the wiggles out. During your praise service, include action and fun songs, too.

Worship music talks *to God*—During the worship songs, not only is the tempo and rhythm different than during the praise songs, but the direction of the words should be pointed upward to God. Worship songs usually contain lyrics that can be personalized. For instance "I love You, Lord"; "God, You're so good to me;" "You are my King."

A good way to help children become more expressive in their worship is to teach them motions to accompany lyrics. When children express themselves physically, the inhibitions they might naturally feel in worshiping God begin to break down.

Looking back at Matthew 21, we see that this chapter begins with Jesus' triumphal entry into Jerusalem, during which a large crowd of people shouted praise and blessings to Jesus. A short while later, children were in the Temple, shouting praises to the Lord. Do you see the correlation? The children were following the examples of their parents!

No matter what you say or do as you lead children into the presence of God, the kids will, in their hearts and minds, still check what you are saying and doing with the example set by their parents. That's one reason it is vital that children have some connection with their parents in a worship service. You might suspend children's church one Sunday per month or once every quarter so families can worship together on Sunday mornings. Follow the Biblical example found in Matthew 21 of parents setting the example of worship for their children.

Jesus Let Children Help Him (John 6:9-11)

Jesus let a young boy get involved in a ministry which led to one of Jesus' greatest recorded miracles—the feeding of the multitude. The boy gave His lunch, and Jesus did the rest.

There is a mighty principle here: allowing children to be active in ministry will nurture their spiritual gifts and callings and bless them as they serve.

What about the children in your ministry? What areas of ministry can you develop to involve and train kids at an early age? Brainstorm how you can create that workforce to help you in your ministry as you train kids for future service in God's kingdom.

In our church on any given Sunday, you will see kids serving on a praise and worship team, performing in our kids' drama team, working on our technical teams, greeting at the doors, opening our kids library, working in our store, praying for one another, ushering and counting the offering, and doing many other things.

Follow the example Jesus set: Let kids help you, involve them in ministry, and watch the ministry multiply!

Jesus Commanded the Feeding of His Lambs (John 21:15-17)

In this passage, as Jesus "reinstates" Peter, He gives him clear direction for the future of the church. Jesus makes it very clear to Peter that He places a priority on ministry to children.

The first time Jesus asks Peter if he loves Him, He tells Peter, "Feed my lambs." The clearest and most straightforward interpretation of lambs is "children." Lambs are not adult sheep, but children.

In the original language, the word *feed* has the following shades of meaning: "tend," "provide pasture for," "take care of," "guide," "govern" and "shepherd."

Our role as ministers to children contains these same elements. We need to care for, discipline, provide facilities for, and lead the lambs God has entrusted to us.

Children in the Church: Covenant Participants

Cheryl Bridges Johns

Will our children be Pentecostal? Will they be Spirit-filled believers who walk before God in holiness of heart, and who pass on to their children our most precious faith?

It is to the Word of God that we turn for answers, not only for what our children are to know, but also how they are to come to know God.

The Scriptures give us both content and process, blending together the *what* and the *how*. Often we focus on the *what*, the content of Scripture, forgetting that the process of *how* we are to know that content and *how* we are to know God is also holy and cannot be separated from His message to us.

The apostle Paul reminded Timothy in 2 Corinthians 1:5 of the faith that was evident in his life. Timothy was the product of sincere faith of the previous generation. Indeed the gift of God that came to Timothy through the laying on of Paul's hands built upon a foundation of a godly mother and grandmother in the context of the New Testament church.

It should be our goal for our children to become living messages of hope, righteousness and belief which are sent into a future that we cannot see. Both the Old and the New Testaments provide for us models as to how we are to send these messages of hope into a future full of uncertainty.

The Old Testament Model

Old Testament scholar Walker Brueggeman sees children as the core of the existence of Israel and as the core of the Torah, the books of the Law. Why was the Law given? So that the children might know God and so continue God's history on the earth. In other words, Israel existed for its children.

The Gift of Children

Psalm 127:3 states that children are a gift from the Lord; therefore, birth was a time of celebration, a time of acknowledging and receiving gifts. First, children were gifts to the parents; second, they were gifts to the community.

Israel did not view children as private possessions of parents; rather, children were part of what Urban Holmes calls "corporate persons" in which the individual embodies the community and the community is responsible for the individual. By this definition people are what they are by virtue of their membership in the community.

In Israel, children were corporate persons of a larger community, not just possessions of two parents. The community owned the children.

Most of all, these children were possessions of a jealous God. For in fact they were representations of His Creator Spirit. Charles Foster reminds us that every child in a sense was *emmanuel*—God with us—and signified hope for the coming One who would be Emmanuel, the "One of God" with us. Therefore, children were God being present among His people. They were God's creative Spirit on the earth.

The Training of Children

In Israel, the naming of children was a special event that placed children in a given context, in a given set of relationships. Thus, the name of a child became his or her most treasured possession, telling a very particular story determined by particular parents and a very particular God. Names were witness to both parentage and to a person's God. Sometimes names would change, as in the case of Abraham and Sarah, to indicate specific action of God on a person's life.

In Israel, then, a named child lived at the very crossroads of the past and future generations. Consequently, it was important for them to go into that future fully prepared.

It is in this context and this backdrop that we read the admonition found in Proverbs 22:6: "Train up a child in the way he should go, and when he is old he will not turn from it." We often interpret this passage through the lens of our own culture in which training is equated with schooling, a formal process of mastering skills and content. However, this verse should be seen against the backdrop of formation in a larger community with particular images of itself and particular images of children.

The Hebrew word which means "to train" literally could mean to initiate, to inaugurate or to consecrate. It is used not only in the Proverbs passage, but in Numbers 7 where the dedication of the altar is referred to; in 1 Kings 8, referring to the dedication of the house of the Lord; and in Ezra 6, dealing with the rebuilding of the Temple. For Israel, children were gifts to be dedicated to God, to be received with joy and lovingly consecrated and initiated into knowledge of God.

How then were children to know God? What processes were involved in their coming to know Him? We see indications of these processes very clearly in Deuteronomy 6:4-9, the Shema, the declaration of Israel's faith in God:

Hear, O Israel: The Lord our God, the Lord is one. Love the Lord your God with all your heart and with all your soul and with all your strength. These commandments that I give you today are to be upon your hearts. Impress them on your children. Talk about them when you sit at home and when you walk along the road, when you lie down and when you get up. Tie them as symbols on your hands and bind them on your foreheads. Write them on the doorframes of your houses and on your gates.

In this passage we see the very heart of Israel's faith—the declaration of who God is and what He expects: a total aligning of the heart toward Him. This knowledge of God was not just to come to the children on special services or special days, but in all of life. God is to be infused in the daily activities of His people. Life is sacred.

The Law of God gave order to this life. He gave order in a world that was in chaos. So the Law gave to Israel a hedge or a fence, a sense of identity in an alien culture that was chaotic. Consequently, children who were born within Israel were born into the Law, were born within the hedge, were born into this ordering of the world. And their lives were to reflect that ordering. They were to know God.

To know God was the ultimate purpose of the Law. From this knowledge derived all other aspects of life. God was to be known in a very intimate way. The Hebrew word for "knowledge" (*yada*) should be understood differently than the way we understand *knowing*, which is, "I know about something—I know the ABC's." But to know God means to be in relationship with Him, to experience Him at the very core of one's being, to center one's life on Him, to totally acknowledge His lordship over every aspect of life. And out of that knowledge comes loving obedience.

So children were not to just know about God, some facts about Him; they were to know God. *Yada* (which was sometimes used as a euphemism for sexual intercourse) indicates an intimate, experiential, covenantal knowledge. The Law was supposed to bring people to a knowledge in which God would be known in covenant. Children were called not to just know about God but to be related to Him and to respond to Him in loving, faithful obedience.

The question then becomes, How do children know God in such a manner that they would be related to Him, aligning their hearts and will according to His purposes? They are to know Him in such a manner that they are to see Him, to respond to Him, to acknowledge Him. Torah gives ways by which the children can attain this knowledge (combining what should be known and how it should be known).

Brueggemann notes that at the heart of the Torah are six questions that are asked not by the adults to the children, but by the children to the adults. These questions are found in the following scriptures:

- Exodus 12:26-27 (the time of the Passover from Egypt): "When your children ask you, 'What does this ceremony mean to you?' then tell them. . . ."
- Exodus 13:8: "On that day tell your son. . . ."
- Exodus 13:14: "In days to come, when your son asks you, 'What does this mean?' say to him. . . ."
- Deuteronomy 6:20-21: "In the future, when your son asks you, 'What is the meaning of the stipulations, decrees and commands the Lord our God has commanded you,' tell him. . . ."
- Joshua 4:6: "In the future, when your children ask you, 'What do these stones mean?' tell them. . . ."
- Joshua 4:21: "In the future, when your descendants ask their fathers, 'What do these stones mean?' tell them. . . ."

Here we have in the life of Israel occasions made to provoke wonder and questioning. In these passages we have flat bread to eat, blood on doorposts, animals being slain, fiery altars, and monuments being erected.

"What does this mean?" ask the children. "Well, then," says the adult, "I'm glad you asked that. Let me tell you a story."

The telling of the story involves more than merely reciting a text. It was to be a testimony—a very personal testimony. It was personal because the person telling the story was part of the history of the event, even though that person may not have lived during the time of the event.

This telling of the story was to be a corporate testimony as well. It was to be a witness of what God had done not only in one's life, but in the life and history of the whole nation. In addition, the story was to be told in such a manner as to invite the children to participate in its continuance.

The story, then, was always open-ended, waiting for the next generation to add another chapter. But those new chapters had to be faithful to those original testimonies, for only in the faithfulness to that original covenant and those original testimonies could the future be insured.

The Future and Children

We have in the Old Testament a God who wants to be known and wants to be loved. And we have a means whereby people can know this God and respond to Him in loving obedience.

God, then, is to be known beyond the present into the future. Hope, therefore, rested in the children. For without the children there is no future. Without the children there is no hope. In each generation that reconciliation equation is to be repeated and made complete. Through this equation children are given a sense of identity and a sense of connection and corporate destiny. (We need to keep the term "corporate destiny" in mind. Do our children today have corporate destiny?)

Summing Up

In the Old Testament, children are to be viewed as gifts from God representing the Spirit of God on the earth. Therefore, they are holy gifts not to be received lightly.

Second, children need to know God, not just know about Him. They may not understand everything, but they can have an active, experiential knowledge of God in their lives.

Third, children are to be trained, lovingly shown the way to God.

Fourth, children are to be shown this way to God by adults who model before them the knowledge of God.

Fifth, children naturally observe this modeling. Hopefully, then, as they observe, they will ask some important questions: "What do you mean by all of this? Why do you live this way?"

Sixth, children need to be ready to testify about God in their own lives; therefore, we have to be ready to testify about God in our lives. We must be ready, instant in season and out. We never know when some child will ask, "What does this mean?" We must have an answer.

Israel was not to say, "Well, we're going to send you down to the priest and they'll tell you all about it." Instead, every adult was to be a teacher of children. Every adult was to be a model. Every adult was to be a caregiver of children. Every adult was to own every child.

This was the ideal—Israel was supposed to live out this model. Many times they did not, but they were held accountable for its standards.

These standards remain for us today.

The New Testament Model

The New Testament provides for us much of this same process of coming to know God. There are differences, however. Knowledge of God is not only to be passed to children, but to adults as well who were formally outside the Torah, or outside the household of faith. So we have adult conversion as a new theme in the life of the church.

In the New Testament we have Torah fulfilled. The full order of God is here revealed in the long-awaited Emmanuel. God is indeed with us through Jesus Christ. And through Jesus Christ we can know (*yada*) God. We can be intimately related to God, reconciled to God.

Christ, therefore, embodied the Law. He did not abolish it, but rather He fulfilled it. He was the one through whom God continued to make history on the earth. Christ's ministry on the earth was one grand occasion of provoking the questions, "What does this mean?" "Who, then, is this, that even the wind and sea obey Him?" "What authority does this man have?" Jesus set Himself up to be asked the questions.

In Christ, gone is the blood on doorposts, but now we have a blood-splattered cross. Gone are the consuming fires on stone altars, and now enters the fire of the Holy Spirit, poured out on our sons and daughters. Gone are the stone monuments. Now we have the living Word and His people who become living stones in the house of God. Children are to be encouraged to meet this Christ, to meet this one full of grace and truth.

Children take a central place in the theme of the kingdom of God through Jesus Christ. They embody the ethics of the kingdom of God. Christ said, "Let the children come to me, and do not hinder them, for the kingdom of God belongs to such as these. I tell you the truth, anyone who will not accept the kingdom of God like a little child will never enter it" (Mark 10:14).

These words were spoken to adults who had a tendency to see children as not adequate or important enough for the kingdom of God. The disciples were constantly amazed at Jesus and had difficulty understanding His agenda. He turns away prime candidates such as the rich young ruler, but He embraces tax collectors and children!

In Christ we see Torah fleshed out, reaching out and embracing the children as it was meant to be from the foundation of the world: God being known to His children who will bear His name. Children, therefore, teach us what it means to be the children of God.

But children! They are messy. They slow you down. They are blunt in their honesty. They are often inarticulate, unpolished in the ways of life. They ask too many questions. They impede on our time. They can't take care of themselves. And they don't even appear to be independent like adults.

The disciples said, "We don't need them. Your kingdom needs to be streamlined." They were on their way to Jerusalem to get God's kingdom established—the coup was going to take place. For the disciples, the kingdom needed to be respectable, polished, and full of power; weakness and dependency did not belong.

Children in the Contemporary Church

This wrong-headed mentality regarding the nature of the kingdom is not limited to the disciples in Jesus' time. Ours is a culture that places little value in children. Our emphasis is on the here and now. Children are an inconvenience.

So we have adult-only communities where we can live apart from the noise and bother of children. Fast disappearing are those close-knit neighborhoods in which children are watched and cared for by not only their parents, but by other adults who love them and take time to reprimand and to care for them. Children now are the exclusive property of parents who live away from extended family members, and who isolate their children from others.

Of course, we have those institutions that take care of our children—safe places—some of which are not so safe. Abuse has taken place even in the best of child-care centers and schools.

We have a society that on one hand pampers children, but on the other hand abuses them. Sometimes these go hand in hand—especially when children are extensions of our ego. It is easy to neglect our children when we view them as our possessions to do with as we please.

Unfortunately, the church sometimes reflects this anti-child bias. We have constructed all-adult worshiping communities, free of noisy, messy, slow, inquisitive children. Here adults can focus on their needs and get their blessing. We want someone else to mind the children. After all, we rationalize, our children are being taught on "their level." Occasionally we may allow our children to entertain us with musicals, but they are not a regular part of our life together.

However, children were the heart of Israel. They are the heart of the Kingdom. But often they are not the heart of the church. In order to bring our children to the heart of the church we must turn our hearts toward them. Children need to see us as incarnate words, living testimonies. We are to be letters of Christ, "written not with ink but with the Spirit of the living God, not on tablets of stone but on tablets of human hearts" (2 Cor. 3:3).

Our children and the unconverted need to see and wonder, "What do these testimonies mean?" "What do you mean by this ceremony?"

We are to evoke such questioning in order that we may respond, "I'm glad you asked. Let me tell you my testimony. For I was an alien, far from God in Egypt, but the Lord delivered me, placed His Spirit on me." The story we tell should indicate a particular identity, showing forth the name of Christ who has given us the gift of life.

For our children to be born again in our communities of faith, they need to understand that they have been named, placed in a community, and that they bear the image of Christ. This name indicates that our eternal life is given to us as a gift to ourselves and to the church. Therefore we are to call our children to be part of the Christian story.

This calling is more than just having altar calls or giving invitations, but it should exist in everyday life. As we go on our way, we are to remember and show forth the praises of Christ. And as signs and wonders follow the believers, our children (and unbelievers) will see and will ask, "What do these things mean?" "Why is this person over here speaking in this strange language?" "Why do we anoint the sick and pray for them?" "Why do we wash feet?" "What is the purpose of Communion?"

It is important to remember that our children are watching our lives. Are we living epistles of the gospel of Jesus Christ? Do we, as the body of Christ, worship for the sake of our children? Are we mature enough to care and to nurture the Pentecostal faith to another generation?

When we begin to honor the little ones among us, we will begin to slow down and allow for a little mess. As we begin to order our lives so that the children will know and love Christ, we will allow for some inconvenience. We do not exist for ourselves or the blessings that we get in our lives, but we exist for the sake of the children and for the unconverted.

As we invite children into our lives, we bring them into the community of the Spirit. And when children come into the community of the Spirit, they come bearing valuable gifts. They can be ministers of the grace of God in ways that adults cannot. They can know God and can be viable members of the church. The household of faith needs children to have hope for the future and have blessings and joy in the present.

This does not mean there are not times when we have our children apart from us for instruction. But we must remember that we can teach religion in a classroom, but we cannot pass on faith outside of a living community of faith.

Too often our children are being taught religion. They may have a lesson on healing and they may learn how Jesus healed the blind man, and they may paste and cut a little figure of a blind man on a little book. But children also need the experience of a powerful worshiping community where healing is a regular occurrence. Such experiences bind us into the Christian story and bring us into a corporate identity.

Finally, it should be noted that children can be filled with the Spirit of God, even though they might not understand the full implications of such an experience. They can know God and they can testify about their knowledge of God.

May we be found faithful in bringing this about for the next generation. May the Lord turn our hearts toward our children. May the Lord bind us to our children, and may we own them and love them. For if we do not, no one else will. And if we do not, they will not have faith.

Life-Changing Children's Leaders

Lance Colkmire & Wilson Kilgore

I've never heard anyone use James 3:1 in their teacher-recruiting efforts. It reads, "Dear brothers and sisters, not many of you should become teachers in the church for we who teach will be judged by God with greater strictness" (NLT).

Teaching God's Word is serious business—especially for those of us who teach children (see Jesus' warning in Matthew 18:6).

However, ministering to children also offers the potential of great reward. Jesus said, "If anyone gives even a cup of cold water to one of these little ones because he is my disciple, I tell you the truth, he will certainly not lose his reward" (Matt. 10:42).

Who Can Minister to Children?

There are four basic qualities an individual needs to be able to minister to children: (1) be compelled by Christ's love, (2) be a burden bearer, (3) know the truth about children's ministry, and (4) be a role model.

Be Compelled by Christ's Love

The compelling love of Christ is the reason to become a children's minister, as seen in 2 Corinthians 5:10-21. This love views children not as brats nor as little angels, but as lost persons in need of the Savior. "Christ's love compels us, because we are convinced that one died for all" (v. 14).

This love sees children as Christ sees them—potential disciples. "So from now on we regard no one from a worldly point of view. . . . If anyone is in Christ, he is a new creation; the old has gone, the new has come!" (vv. 16-17).

Christ's love drives one to pray, "Give me Your heart, O God! Give me the ministry of bringing boys and girls to You." God has "committed to us the message of reconciliation. We are therefore Christ's ambassadors, as though God were making his appeal through us" (vv. 19-20).

Love realizes that even boys and girls can become "the righteousness of God" (v. 21).

Be a Burden Bearer

"I've lost my burden for these kids" is the parting statement of countless teachers when they resign. When I hear those words, I want to ask . . .

Do you really know what a burden is?

- Did you *ever* have a burden for this class?
- Have you asked God to give you a burden or to renew your burden for those children?

What Is a Burden? Three different nouns translate as *burden* in the New Testament.

The one we are concerned with here (*baros*) refers to something heavy, something pressing. It makes a demand on one's physical, material, and/or spiritual resources.

Christ carried this kind of burden for us. His burden cost Him materially as He gave up the glory of heaven; spiritually, as He bore our sins and was separated from His father. Jesus called this His "cup" as He prayed in Gethsemane. It overwhelmed His soul "with sorrow to the point of death" (Matt. 26:38). He asked His closest disciples to help Him carry this burden by praying with Him. But while Jesus' whole being was crushed for the souls of humanity, His disciples' eyes were burdened ("heavy") with sleep! So Jesus prayed alone, "My Father, if it is not possible for this cup to be taken away unless I drink it, may your will be done" (v. 42).

Today, Jesus is still seeking disciples who are willing to give of themselves in whatever way necessary to serve the needs of others. He's looking for burden bearers.

What Is Our Responsibility? There's an apparent contradiction about burden bearing in Galatians 6. Verse 2 says, "Bear ye one another's burdens," but verse 5 reads, "For every man shall bear his own burden" (KJV). Which is it?

The word translated as "burden" in verse 5 is *phortion*, which refers to something that an individual can carry. (A better translation is "load.") The message is that each Christian is personally responsible for carrying his own cross—for fulfilling the mission to which Christ has called him.

That's good news for children's leaders. God will not hold us accountable for the way our kids respond (or fail to respond) to Christ's call to discipleship. We cannot, nor must we try to, do for our kids what God calls them to do for themselves.

At the same time, verse 2 commands us to put our shoulder alongside our children's shoulders when they have "burdens" (*baros*) that are too heavy for them to bear alone. In so doing, the verse continues, we will "fulfill the law of Christ"—the law that says we must love others as we love ourselves.

When our students have spiritual, physical, or material needs, we are to let Christ burden our heart so we might help meet those needs. We will be held accountable for our obedience to the command, "Bear ye one another's burdens."

Do We Have Compassion? Compassion is the mark of a teacher who is burdened for his or her students.

Over and over, the Bible says Jesus was "moved with compassion" when He saw someone in need. This doesn't mean Jesus simply felt sorry for them. Instead, the heaviness of their needs actually pressed on Christ's vital organs and on His spirit. He felt what they felt, and more!

If you do not have that kind of compassion for your students, follow the advice Charles Stanley gives in his book *Handle With Prayer*:

"Tell God you are willing to be part of the answer. Then ask Him to share their burden with you. Ask God for a real spirit of love and compassion. Tell Him you want Him to teach you how to pray and intercede on their behalf."

Know the Truth

A children's minister laughs at the following three myths about children's ministry:

1. *Teaching kids is easier than teaching adults, right?* Sure—except for discipline issues, short attention spans, the variety of activities needed, unconcerned parents, and so on.

2. *Children have a simple level of faith and understanding, so their leaders do not have to know much, right?* Exactly! The faith questions kids ask are softies like these: Where is heaven? Why did God let my mom get cancer? Where did God come from?

The truth is that a children's pastor or teacher must be a student of the Word and be able to translate spiritual truths into kid talk.

3. *The leader's spiritual level is unimportant if he likes kids and relates well, right?* Actually, the leader must be a growing Christian who loves kids and who humbles himself to see things as children see them.

Be a Christian Role Model

The writer of Hebrews said, "Remember your leaders . . . who brought to you the Word of God. Observe attentively and consider their manner of living—the outcome of their well-spent lives—and imitate their faith" (13:7 AMP).

That scripture sums up the kind of role model that a children's leader should be.

The Ministry of the Children's Pastor

Children are indeed blessed when they have someone they can call their own pastor. A children's pastor is an advocate, a shepherd, an administrator, a soulwinner, and a worship leader.

An Advocate

A children's pastor becomes an advocate for the children in his or her church. This person brings the needs of children to the pastor, church council, and congregation. He or she also provides the leadership and planning necessary to address the needs of children in the church and community.

While not usurping the lead pastor's responsibilities to the little ones in his flock, the children's pastor becomes a vital ministry extension.

A Shepherd

Elsie Lippy wrote, "Pastoring children means suffering on their behalf" (*Evangelizing Today's Child*). It means suffering "the pain of aloneness required for effectual, fervent prayer for children . . . [and spending] hours alone in God's Word to develop a life-changing lesson." It means undergoing "the pain of involvement . . . to bear the suffering of our children." It means enduring "the weariness of well doing."

The shepherding duties of the children's pastor can be summarized in six statements:

1. Pray consistently for the children.
2. Cultivate strong relationships with them.
3. Provide spiritual counsel.
4. Help parents to become spiritual shepherds in their own homes.
5. Be a spiritual leader for the children.
6. Develop solid relationships with the children's workers and be a spiritual leader for them.

An Administrator

Integrating. The children's pastor must cause the children's department to operate like an orchestra instead of like a mismatched collage of instruments. There should be a balance between the four crucial elements of church life: instruction, worship, fellowship, and service.

The children's pastor should list all the active kids programs by age level. Next, list what is going on in each program during the present quarter, and what is planned for the next quarter. Then ask: Are needs being met? Is there a balance? Is there redundancy? Is something missing?

Once the children's pastor determines the needs, he or she works with departmental leaders in deciding where changes need to be made and in implementing those changes.

Getting help. Finding and training workers is the natural follow-up to discovering where children's ministry is lacking. Specific training should be given to help meet specific needs.

Developing a calendar. Listing all of the dates for regularly scheduled children's programs and special events will help the children's pastor to oversee a balanced program. A calendar will also help to avoid conflicts with other church ministries. Too, it will keep church leaders and members informed about children's ministries.

Leading special events. The children's pastor oversees special events such as Vacation Bible School, harvest festival, Easter celebration, and so on.

A Soulwinner

A children's pastor provides leadership in winning children to Christ. In his article "Evangelizing Little Children," Ralph Williams points out four reasons why conversion of children is so important:

1. Win a child and you save a life.
2. Many of the greatest men [and women] of God were converted in early childhood.
3. It is much easier to win a child than an adult to Christ.
4. Converted children are among the most useful workers for Christ (from the *Encyclopedia of Evangelism*).

A Preparer for Worship

A children's pastor helps prepare children for meaningful participation in congregational worship. While taking full advantage of children's church ministry, he is careful to fight the out-of-sight, out-of-mind syndrome. In too many churches children are almost always in separate classes and worship experiences. Dick

Gruber calls this "parallel child care." He laments, "We are, in practice, raising a general of potential church dropouts. These children have never experienced a multi-generational worship service" (*Children's Church: Turning Your Circus Into a Service*).

The children's pastor should help children discover, experience, and practice worship in kids church. At the same time, he or she should make sure the children are part of congregational worship on a regular basis. In some churches, kids are part of the corporate worship service until the preaching time, when they go to kids church. In other churches, there is no kids church once each month.

The Ministry of the Children's Teacher

If you're a children's teacher, you've probably caught yourself echoing one of Solomon's proverbs: "My sons, listen to me; pay attention to what I say" (Prov. 7:24).

"Kids, listen to me! Pay attention to what I'm saying!" is the battle cry of countless children's teachers.

So how do you as a children's teacher do it? You've got the most important message in the world to communicate, but how can you get your kids to zero in on what you're teaching?

Give Them Your Attention

King Solomon's son Rehoboam—heir to the throne—did not heed his dad's counsel, and his life came to ruin. Why? The main problem was King Solomon—he did not live according to the God-given wisdom he himself laid out in Proverbs. Instead, he was a hypocrite!

As a children's teacher, *the starting point in gaining your students' attention is earning their respect.* Only if you're living by the principles you're teaching will your students listen to you.

Another problem Solomon probably had was in giving proper attention to Rehoboam. With the king having 700 wives, 300 concubines, the world's greatest stash of riches and the world's mightiest army to take care of, it's unlikely that the prince saw much of him.

That brings us to the next principle: *before your students will pay attention to you, you must pay attention to them.* What are some ways you can get involved in your children's lives?

INSIDE THE CLASSROOM
1. Make a habit of getting to class early or staying a few minutes late for a time of "planned informality."
2. Listen closely to, remember, and pray for the children's prayer requests. Also have them help you pray for *your* needs.

3. Periodically conduct surveys. Have students write out answers to questions about their spiritual and personal lives.
4. Talk about your own life experiences.
5. Plan activities that will affirm your students' value as individuals made in God's image.

OUTSIDE THE CLASSROOM
1. Send students cards with personal notes—on birthdays, at Christmas, when they have been absent, and when they have special needs.
2. Conduct fun events for them.
3. Give their parents your phone number, inviting them to call when their child has a prayer need.
4. Plan and carry out ministry projects as a group.

Another step in giving your students proper attention is *lesson preparation*. Have your students in mind as you prayerfully and deliberately prepare your lesson. Determine what single truth should be the lesson focus, and write it down. For instance:

- Ask, "Has anyone ever made fun of you because of your beliefs?"
- Show a photo which depicts someone being bullied.
- Have kids do a role play in which students are making fun of one of their peers.

The introduction must harness the students' thoughts and point them toward the lesson focus.

Keeping Their Attention

Once you have your students' attention, the challenge is *keeping* it. When you are talking, maintain interest by varying your voice, changing your position in the room, using eye contact, using vocabulary they understand, saying the unexpected, asking questions, showing emotions.

Involve the students' five senses as much as possible. For instance, when teaching on Christ's temptation, bring bread for them to smell and taste. When teaching that Christ was crucified, bring a sharp nail and a thorny plant for students to touch.

Use creative methods that kids enjoy—role play, mime, stories, object lessons, projects, games—to effectively communicate the day's message.

Finally, rephrase the lesson truth into a pointed, personalized statement at the end. For example, "Are you born again? If not, God can change you as He changed Nicodemus." Then challenge them to respond.

As you give, gain, and keep attention, may God give your children the grace to heed one of Solomon's final wise words: "Remember your Creator in the days of your youth" (Eccl. 12:1 NKJV).

Building a Team: Recruiting, Equipping, and Keeping Volunteers

Cindy Hunnicutt

I'm a children's pastor, called to bring the good news of Jesus to boys and girls. . . . And now I learn I have to be a recruiter, trainer, public-relations specialist, and salesperson too?"

Yes, children's pastor, God has called you to a big role, and with reliance on the Lord, you can do it! Our mission is not only to reach children but also to be a beacon of light to adults, highlighting the importance of ministry to the special treasure God has given us in our kids.

First John 5:3-5 shows us that our faith motivates God to help us in any area of need—including recruitment of ministry staff:

Loving God means keeping his commandments, and his commandments are not burdensome. For every child of God defeats this evil world, and we achieve this victory through our faith. And who can win this battle against the world? Only those who believe that Jesus is the Son of God (NLT).

God can prosper your ministry efforts regardless of where you live, who you are, or the resources you possess. It begins with your loving God and obeying Him with all your heart. "If you listen to these commands of the Lord your God that I am giving you today, and if you carefully obey them, the Lord will make you the head and not the tail, and you will always be on top and never at the bottom" (Deut. 28:13 NLT).

We children's pastors offer an amazing opportunity and privilege to those we recruit to serve alongside us. We attract potential workers by helping them catch a vision of using their gifts and skills to make an authentic spiritual impact in the lives of children. We also afford workers the opening to be blessed and rewarded by God. Proverbs 19:17 says, "If you help the poor, you are lending to the Lord—and he will repay you!" (NLT).

Although our kids may or may not be *poor* in the financial sense of the word, they certainly need adults to help them learn God's Word and discern His voice. Volunteers can help fulfill that need in a child's life—and the Lord will repay them for their ministry to His kids!

Learn how to communicate your vision for children's ministry within your church and to potential volunteers. Don't keep it a secret. Open your heart to your workers by making your vision for children's ministry plain. Give your folks (and your pastor) bragging ammo for all the good things God is doing through your workers. The Lord says to us "Write my answer on a billboard, large and clear, so that anyone can read it at a glance and rush to tell others" (in Hab. 2:2 TLB).

Vision is the motivating factor in attracting and keeping workers on your team. We want potential workers to be able to understand our vision easily and rush to get involved. People must be brought together to be productive. Casting your vision for the importance and excitement of serving in children's ministry allows a team to begin to form around your vision and generates a desire to be involved. How can that be done?

Pray

Keep your entire children's ministry—workers, parents, and kids—aware of and praying for your staffing needs. Widen the pool of potential recruits by involving more folks in the recruitment process. Ask everyone involved in children's ministry to pray for and suggest names of folks they know to serve alongside them. Our job is to pray, not attempt to motivate potential workers with guilt!

Jesus said to His disciples, "The harvest is great, but the workers are few. So pray to the Lord who is in charge of the harvest; ask him to send more workers into his fields" (Matt. 9:37-38 NLT).

Position

Make expectations and descriptions clear of what positions are available. Create job descriptions for every possible opening in your ministry. God has promised in Philippians 4:19 to meet all your needs, so list them all! Break the jobs into small pieces whenever possible. Identify the gifts and abilities needed for that position. Allow your ministry openings to fit into the lifestyles and time available to those whom you are recruiting.

Prospects

Always be on the lookout for prospects to join you in ministry. Listen to people as they speak, determining their interests and passions. Find a place in ministry that would allow them to use their gifts and talents in a way that is fulfilling to the call on their lives. Don't just try to "fill holes."

When Jesus recruited, He drafted. He didn't wait for the fishermen to come to Him, He told them to follow. And they did! He also called disciples one or two at a time. And some of those disciples recruited others. Andrew brought Simon to Jesus, and Philip brought Nathanael (John 1:40-45).

Don't be discouraged by recruitment of just one or two workers at a time. Encourage your team to recruit folks from their circle of influence. Ask people you meet in the church how they are engaged and where they are serving. If they are not serving anywhere else, draft them. Tell them you need them in the children's ministry, and then repeat step 1—pray!

Personalize

Personally contact your prospects. Meet them in the hallway at church. Send them an email of introduction. Call them to make an appointment to chat. Help them hear your heart for ministry. Cast a compelling vision. It's hard to turn down someone face-to-face.

If you are recruiting a large number of volunteers for a special or seasonal event, it may not be possible to meet each person one-on-one. However, a brief after-church meeting or coffee-and-doughnuts meeting before church, where you can meet in person with several potential volunteers at one time, can still provide the necessary personal touch needed in recruitment.

Provide

Once a person expresses interest in joining your team, provide them a chance to observe the ministry in action before making the final decision. This will help the new recruit understand the ministry better and help you best place the person for fulfilling their ministry goals.

Make a follow-up contact with your prospect for an answer. Accept their decision. Be gracious if their answer is no. However, when the answer is yes, quickly provide orientation and the tools they need to begin their ministry with success.

Equip Your Volunteers

What shapes the relationships among the workers on your team? Meetings or memories? Creating memories as we serve the Lord together shoulder to shoulder is more powerful and strengthening than another meeting on the calendar. However, training and equipping are important pieces in developing that team that can create memories and share experiences together. Here are a few tips:

Once a worker has said yes, have them complete the required paperwork, and then do a background check. Two possible sources for background checks are "Shepherd's Watch" (*www.group.com*) and *protectmyministry.com*.

After the volunteer has been cleared to serve, schedule a time of orientation as soon as possible. The orientation might include these pieces:

- Tour of the facilities (*Where is the copy machine? Where are the first-aid kits?*)
- Restroom procedures and policies
- How do I check in? Is there a name tag I must wear?
- What is the dress code for a worker?
- What are the church membership requirements?
- Who do I contact if I will be late or absent?
- What and how do I prepare for my ministry role?
- Where are the supplies? How do I access them?
- Is there reimbursement for any expenses I incur?
- When can I come to set up my room? Will my room already be set up for me?
- Is there curriculum? How do I access it?
- What are the safety policies and procedures?
- Do I have a co-leader? Is this a small-group or large-group setting?
- Think through the steps a worker will walk through in preparation for and actually doing the work of the ministry. Anticipate those questions and give those answers at the orientation. We also include a small gift at orientation as we welcome workers to our team.

One of the best ways to train a volunteer is to put them with someone who is already trained and successful in the ministry. Serving alongside a seasoned volunteer allows for personal, one-on-one training that group meetings, online videos, and memos cannot reproduce.

Hold annual retreats or daylong experiences where you can pour out your heart and vision for the ministry to your workers. Allow them to hear your vision up close. Pray together and play together at this event. It's amazing what can come from a few focused hours together.

Provide resources to leaders whenever possible: online training, articles, and/or books that will enhance their ministry abilities, along with CDs/podcasts to listen to during drive time.

Keep 'Em!

Spend time with your folks. Jesus invested Himself into a group of twelve men for over three years by teaching them, traveling the countryside with them, and involving Himself in their lives. He healed Peter's mother, loved John, corrected them when necessary, ate and fellowshipped with them, washed their feet, prayed with them, and allowed them to serve alongside Him in the ministry. Jesus' example is for us too.

Make regular opportunities to speak with your folks personally as often as you can. Pray with them so they can hear your heart and you can hear theirs. Show concern and follow up when they express difficulties in their personal lives. Rejoice when good things happen for them and their family members. Become the go-to person who celebrates and mourns alongside with them.

Pastor your flock of workers. Say "thank you." Send your team birthday cards and thank-you notes. Give them small gifts, highlight them in front of your kids and in written communication to parents. Make heroes of your volunteers and they will stick with you for the long haul.

Also, have fun! Plan regular opportunities to socialize with your team. Create memories together. A meal after church, a weekend retreat, attending their family events when possible—all these go a long way into increasing the bond between you and your workers. People want to belong. Be your workers' friend.

Suggested Resources

Big Book of Job Descriptions (Gospel Light) includes descriptions for positions from executive pastor to cookie baker, from administrative assistant to puppeteer, from usher to pantry organizer. Besides the job descriptions, you may discover a ministry you might never have thought of and expand your ministry in the process! Reproducible CD-ROM included.

Volunteers That Stick (Jim Wideman, Group Publishing) offers the secrets of retention through other ideas that really work. Instill leadership skills and grow your church volunteers to be happy, inspired, and in it for the long haul.

Teacher Training on the Go (Group Publishing) will help you train (and retrain) volunteers. A year's worth of reproducible training handouts helps volunteers be their best. Their skills and effectiveness in children's ministry will grow.

Take-Out Training for Teachers (Group Publishing) helps you reach training goals without scheduling a single meeting, and with minimal prep time. Fifty-two engaging training sessions draw the most out of your teachers with principles they can apply immediately.

Financing Ministry to Children

Irma Hendrix

"We've got plenty of great ideas . . . but how do we get money to put those ideas into action?"

OK, got the question. Now let's do some soul-searching for your children's ministry. This will involve prayer, more questions, prayer, evaluating, more prayer, work, prayer . . . and then God-directed answers will be evident.

By praying at the beginning, you will not waste time or energy on meaningless side trips. Also, ask some pointed questions of yourself and the children's ministry. Those questions may include these:

- Does your pastor and church place value on children's ministry as a genuine ministry? If not, how are you to working to change this perspective?
- Is the church willing to partner with you in developing the best programs for the children?

It is expensive to minister to children—it is a ministry of blessing and sowing that involves money, time, talent and lots of dedication.

- Are you communicating the vision of your children's ministry to the pastor, church, parents and children?

Evaluation is the next step. If this area is a struggle for you, enlist some help. Answer the following questions:

- What ministries are being offered?

- What are the number and the ages of children taking part in those ministries?
- What are the current needs of those programs?

Next, what are the goals of the children's ministry? What tools are needed to help reach those goals?

The catalyst to spark the actions needed as a result of your evaluation and goal-setting is prayer. "Dream the impossible dream." God is a big God—He will honor your faith. Put your faith into action: "Now faith is being sure of what we hope for and certain of what we do not see" (Heb. 11:1).

The following story, which has been widely circulated on the Internet, tells how one girl put her faith into action:

The Price of a Miracle

Tess was a precocious eight-year-old when she heard her Mom and Dad talking about her little brother, Andrew. All she knew was that he was very sick and they were out of money. He needed a very costly surgery, and it was looking like there was no one to loan them the money. She heard Daddy say to her tearful Mother with whispered desperation, "Only a miracle can save him now."

Tess went to her bedroom and pulled a glass jelly jar from its hiding place in the closet. She poured all the change out on the floor and counted it carefully. The total had to be exactly perfect. No chance here for mistakes. Carefully placing the coins back in the jar and twisting on the cap, she slipped out the back door and made her way six blocks to the local drugstore. She waited patiently for the pharmacist to give her some attention but he was too busy. Tess twisted her feet to make a scuffing noise. Nothing. So she cleared her throat with the most disgusting sound she could muster. No good

Finally she took a quarter from her jar and banged it on the glass counter. That did it!

"And what do you want?" the pharmacist asked in an annoyed tone of voice. "I'm talking to my brother from Chicago whom I haven't seen in ages," he said without waiting for a reply to his question.

"Well, I want to talk to you about *my* brother," Tess answered back in the same annoyed tone. "He's really sick . . . and I want to buy a miracle."

"I beg your pardon?" said the pharmacist.

"His name is Andrew and he has something bad growing inside his head and my daddy says only a miracle can save him now. So, how much does a miracle cost?"

"We don't sell miracles here, little girl. I'm sorry, but I can't help you," the pharmacist said, softening a little.

"Listen, I have the money to pay for it. If it isn't enough, I will get the rest. Just tell me how much it costs."

The pharmacist's brother was a well-dressed man. He stooped down and asked the little girl, "What kind of a miracle does your brother need?"

"I don't know," Tess replied with her eyes welling up. "I just know he's really sick and Mommy says he needs an operation. But Daddy can't pay for it, so I want to use my money."

"How much do you have?" asked the man from Chicago.

"One dollar and eleven cents," Tess whispered. "And it's all the money I have, but I can get some more if I need to."

"Well, what a coincidence," smiled the man. "A dollar and eleven cents—the exact price of a miracle for little brothers." He took her money in one hand and with the other hand he grasped her mitten and said, "Take me to where you live. I want to see your brother and meet your parents. Let's see if I have the kind of miracle you need."

That man was a neurosurgeon. The operation was completed without charge, and it wasn't long until Andrew was home again and doing well. Mom and Dad were happily talking about the chain of events that had led them to this place.

"That surgery," her Mom whispered, "was a real miracle. I wonder how much it would have cost?"

Tess smiled. She knew exactly how much a miracle cost: one dollar and eleven cents, plus the faith of a little child.

A miracle is not the suspension of natural law, but the operation of a higher law.

Read that last line again: "A miracle is not the suspension of a natural law, but the operation of a higher law."

Seek, Knock, Ask

A great plan to follow for gaining the finances needed for ministry is as easy as 1, 2, 3. It is founded on the Biblical principle of "ask, seek and knock" (Matt. 7:7).

1. *Seek and identify the specific areas of needs.* Compose a list of those needs according to the importance of the items, and place them on a visual timeline. This places the dreams on paper for all to see and will give you a reference point as God starts to fulfill those needs.

Look for unconventional ways to get supplies. If you do not have the time to do the extra seeking, enlist some of your parents or volunteers to help in the hunt.

Garage sales. I take about $30 with me, a few tax-contribution receipts, my church business card, and a tablet or receipt book to record items purchased for the ministry.

Scavenger hunt. Enlist staff members, parents, and church family to help. Make a list of needed items and give out your "wish list" for everyone to check their attics and garages for donations to children's ministries.

Dumpsters behind large department stores. Get permission from the manager before "dumpster diving." Most of the time they will be glad to hold tossed-out items for you.

Curbside "recyclying." If your local government provides curbside pick-up for residents discarding large items, you'd be amazed at what you can find. If your area does this, you can learn the day of the pick-up route. Hours before the scheduled pick-ups, go treasure hunting. It's wise to let a homeowner know you are taking an item. You might leave your ministry card on their door with a note saying what you have taken.

2. *Knock on the doors already available to you.*

On the Internet, search sites for information on the products or services you need.

Check for free products from local, district, and national distributors.

Keep your eyes open for displays at your local stores that can be used in the ministry. Leave your number with a manager and ask him or her to call you when the store is discarding the display.

3. *Ask in faith, and it will be given to you.*

Compose a letter requesting a donation on church stationery. If possible, meet with the local manager of the store or company to request your needs, and leave the letter. When a donation is made, make sure a note of thanks is sent promptly to the company.

Advertise for items you currently need by using the church bulletin and/or website and by communicating with parents.

Give to Receive

There is an important Biblical principle in Luke 6:38 that must be understood: "Give and it will be given to you. A good measure, pressed down, shaken together and running over, will be poured into your lap. For with the measure you use, it will be measured to you." Give extra money, supplies, and ideas from your children's ministry to another ministry or missionary. Make the commitment to do this on a regular basis. Also, don't be a packrat; instead, use strategic planning for all your events and classes. Plan ahead. God will help you get the needed resources if you know what you want and use those resources wisely.

Teaching Stewardship

Boys and girls who understand "Jesus loves me" are ready to know the basics of tithing and giving. They also need to know that giving to Jesus involves more than money. They should give of their praise and worship, their talents, time, and energy.

There are many ways to make this learning fun and memorable. A starting point is to always read a scripture before receiving an offering to remind the children that we give because the Bible commands it.

Placing little church banks in the preschool room entrance helps parents to join in the giving experience with their children.

For children's worship, you can use an offering-contest machine. Build a scale that will show by weight or sight the winner of each offering taken. Each unit of money is represented by a weight or visual token. Usually the teams are boys versus girls. It really gets exciting when the teams have a target amount to achieve and the adults get involved.

Kids like to give to a cause or project. Display a picture or model of how the money is going to be used. Make sure you get the information to the kids' families a few weeks before the contest begins. This will promote excitement and involvement.

Fundraisers

Fundraisers are a great way to generate income for your ministry and promote community among families. However, do not overload families and yourself by doing fundraiser after fundraiser. This will exhaust you and have parents saying, "Not something else to sell!" Remember that their children are involved with other organizations—such as schools, sports programs, and scouting—that also do fundraisers.

When you do a fundraising event, make it count for the building of the child and family by involving Scripture verses and goals to help them learn more about God. This will take a little more creative time, but it is worth it.

Following are several types of fundraisers:

An annual *white elephant sale* held in your church parking lot or the large yard of a church member.

Silent auctions for themed baskets or original art work done by the kids. This is a wonderful way to showcase the kids' God-given talents.

Crafts or professional services with all the profits going to the children's ministry. Portraits, craft fairs, booths, pet grooming, and food coupons are a few ideas.

Dessert theater with a children's talent show or fashion show (with kids' clothing sponsored by a local children's boutique). This is a great church community builder and talent spotlight.

Bible memorization or quiz teams that raise money from sponsors depending on the number of scriptures they memorize or how long they can last without losing in a Scripture quiz. This has long-lasting benefits for the kids who memorize Bible verses.

King and queen, prince and princess. Designate a month for the kids to raise money any way they can. The boy and girl who raise the most money will be named king and queen, while the second-place finishers will be named prince and princess. The winners are given crowns and receive special privileges. For instance, they will not have to pay for any activity the children's department sponsors throughout the year.

Marathons. Kids love to participate in rock-a-thons, bike-a-thons, walk-a-thons, read-a-thons, and similar events. Sponsors agree to pay participants a certain amount per hour, per mile, per book, or per whatever other criterion is established.

Baked goods auction. Let the kids bring baked goods they have made (with the help of parents, hopefully) to be sold at an after-church auction. Besides raising funds, it's a fun family event.

Yardsticks of quarters. Distribute yardsticks. Challenge the kids to collect quarters and tape them to the yardstick, covering both sides. Then they bring the yardsticks back to church. You'll raise about $25 for each completed yardstick.

Shower of gifts. If your nursery needs a new changing table or rocking chair . . . and if your kindergarten class needs new puzzles or curtains . . . and if you need handbells to start a handbell choir . . . and if your kids church needs a new electronic gizmo . . . let people know. Have a "shower" for your kids ministry one Saturday or Sunday afternoon, when church members will donate those items.

I'm sure you and your workers have many more ideas that will work amazingly for your church and children. In whatever you do, let God be in charge. It is His ministry, and He wants you to manage it with Biblical stewardship. He already has all the resources and will direct you to them or direct the resources to you. Pray and believe while you go about doing your best for His kingdom and the church of today—children. "Trust in the Lord with all your heart and lean not on your own understanding; in all your ways acknowledge him, and he will make your paths straight" (Prov. 3:5-6).

Reaching the "In Between" Preteens

Cindy Hunnicutt & Keith Wilson

Active, curious, cooperative . . . active, friendly, verbal, easygoing . . . active, agreeable, fun . . . and active! Ten- and eleven-year-olds are special people.

The advent of middle school has ushered our preteens into the teen scene earlier than ever, exposing them to sophisticated ideas and behaviors. However, today's fifth and sixth graders are not necessarily more grown-up than preteens of earlier generations. So what can the church provide that will minister especially to this in-between age group?

The church should endeavor to provide a strong spiritual network for these kids, as well as a strong social program to help develop friendships. The purpose should be to minister to kids and hold them in church during the rapid-change preteen and adolescent years. It is vital that kids be planted—to have an attachment with Christian friends and church life—before they leave our children's ministry and move on to the youth group.

Giving Preteens a Place to Belong

Most churches offer programs such as Sunday school, kids church, midweek clubs. Try to update these ministries. For instance, our Sunday school has reformatted the fifth- and sixth-grade class. Hands-on, active learning—which involves role-plays, skits, and group projects—is taking place.

We also offer more grown-up opportunities to show fifth and sixth graders they are recognized as preteens instead of children. We have divided preteens into "families" for small-group interaction and care for one another. These groups provide a niche for belonging, nurture and friendship.

Monthly Specials

We schedule a monthly special activity for fifth and sixth graders. We offer a home Bible study one month, a social event the next month, and continue that pattern throughout the year. Bible studies can begin with playing games and eating snacks. Then spend time in family groups talking about personal concerns, praying together, and studying God's Word.

Social activities can include the tried and true: bowling, miniature golf, and eating out. However, you may like to come up with some more ambitious socials from time to time. We once spent a summer day at Six Flags over Georgia (Don't you think that would have been enough for one day?), then traveled to one of our leaders' homes to swim, play volleyball, and "relax" from our day at Six Flags. Later that night we went to the church and played indoor hide-and-seek. Next, our "families" talked and prayed together. Finally it was video time, during which most of the kids eventually went to sleep until time to go home.

On one New Year's Eve we went out to eat and play games at a pizza-and-game place. We then returned to church for a crazy scavenger hunt through the darkened building with flashlights. After that, we played some wild games with newspaper. Then we settled down to receive Communion and pray together as midnight approached. What a way to start the New Year!

Preteens in Ministry

God has always used children to accomplish His will. Take a look at how God used young Samuel to confront Eli (1 Sam. 3). Or how about the service rendered by the boy king Josiah, whom God put in place (2 Kings 22)? Someone must have done a good job training the servant girl of Naaman's wife, for she spoke boldly to her unbelieving master (2 Kings 5). Of course, we're all familiar with the boy who gave the loaves and fish with which Jesus performed one of His greatest miracles.

In our church, we give preteens regular opportunities to serve. We hold a monthly training session during which they're instructed how to serve on a ministry team. We train in these areas: ushering, drama, prayer, greeting, praise and worship, technical support, puppetry, and others. Completing the training qualifies a preteen to minister in that capacity in kids church.

On the first Sunday many years ago when our kids were allowed to minister, there was electricity in the air. You could feel it! Both kids and adults were so excited to see children praying for the offering and then receiving it. When the prayer team of children came to the altar at prayer time and laid hands on their friends, it was obvious they were touching the heart of God.

Our preteen puppet team ministers in our preschool department every Sunday. The preschool leaders tell us the highlight of Sunday morning begins when they line up the toddlers' chairs in preparation for our preteen puppeteers' visit to their classroom.

In our kids church we have a boy who has attention deficit disorder, is hyperactive, and has a behavior disorder. He wanted to serve on our technical team, running our lights and projector. Although the leader was somewhat hesitant, we did accept him on this team, and he was trained in that capacity. Much to the leader's surprise and to the boy's excitement, he has done a marvelous job! He focuses on his job, pays attention to cues, and stays on task. His mother told us he can't wait to get to church on Sunday mornings to do his job because it makes him feel important.

In our ministry, we try to train children in various areas of Christian service in which we would eventually like for them to be involved as teens and adults. For example, before our annual kids crusade, we take our fifth and sixth graders door-to-door and to shopping centers to hand out fliers advertising our upcoming event. When we turn our kids loose (with adult leaders nearyby), they become mini-evangelists, talking to everyone they encounter and inviting them to our church. They are learning boldness and gaining experience in telling others about God and the church.

Graduation Banquet

The highlight of the year in our preteen ministry is our sixth-grade graduation banquet. This is a big event, held at the end of the summer, in which our sixth graders and their parents are served a banquet. We hold the dinner at church, which we decorate according to the chosen theme. Invitations are sent out, tickets are sold, and we even print a program. Our current and rising fifth graders serve the meal and provide entertainment.

Entertainment might include songs and skits which gently poke fun at the graduating sixth graders. Once we presented tongue-in cheek Candy Awards to each sixth grader. For instance, our shortest girl received the "Hershey Kiss Award" because good things come in small packages. We also put the seventh-grade Sunday school teachers and our youth pastor on the program to greet and speak to the rising youth.

A highlight of the evening is a video trip down memory lane featuring our graduates. Such a video brings laughter and tears to the kids and parents alike. We end with a closing prayer and blessing as we send our graduating sixth graders on to the youth group. Each graduate receives a Bible promise book as well as a photo of themselves at the banquet.

A Place to Belong

Our preteen ministry has been so important in giving our kids an identity and a place to belong as they are challenged to make lifetime commitments to the

Lord. As one fifth grader (who had recently moved to our church from another state) said with tears in her eyes, "At first I didn't want to move, but now I have so many friends here. This is where I belong."

Teaching Preteens a Lesson

Preteens learn best through what they do and see.

In an average class of 10 sixth-grade students, it would be normal to find two auditory, four visual, and four tactile/kinesthetic [hands-on] learners. Unfortunately for eight out of ten of our students, 90 percent of all teaching is auditory. The teaching processes most often used by teachers are lecture, storytelling, questions and answer, and discussion (Youthworker Update).

To teach preteens successfully, we must make our lessons as hands-on, interactive, and visual as we can. We should also follow a four-step teaching approach:

1. *Seeing the Need.* Preteens usually come to church with their minds on everything except the study of God's Word. That's why teachers must not hit them cold with an opening statement like "Today we will be studying about an Old Testament prophet named Jeremiah." Instead, the wise teacher will capture the students' interest by using an introduction that speaks to his students where they live; then the teacher will tie that introduction into the subject at hand. This will cause students to think, *Today's lesson is for me!*

2. *Searching the Word.* Here are three keys to successful Bible study with preteens:
   - Using a variety of methods—the more hands-on and visual, the better
   - Letting the kids discover Bible truths for themselves
   - Spending about 50 percent of the class time on Bible study, leaving plenty of time for application and response.

3. *Applying the Word.* Teaching Bible stories and Bible facts is not enough. Teachers also must help students answer the "so what?" question. God gave Moses 10 engraved laws—so what? God made Adam and Eve—so what? The aim is to help preteens discover how the day's scriptural focus speaks to them.

4. *Acting on the Word.* In this final step, students should be challenged to do something specific with the message they have just heard. Of course, the role of the Holy Spirit is vital here, "for it is God who works in you to will and to act according to his good purpose" (Phil. 2:13).

Following are a couple of lessons for preteens that are based on this model.

Breaking Sinful Habits

The goal of this lesson is to help preteens understand sin's effects and seek God's power to help them overcome sinful habits.

Seeing the Need. You will be the master in a game called "Obey the Master." The students will be slaves. Explain that this game is a little bit like Simon Says. The slaves will try to gain their freedom. To do this, they must perfectly obey five of your commands in a row. Each time they do not correctly follow a command, they must start over.

Give two or three commands they can easily follow (such as "Clap your hands," "Touch your toes," and so on). Then give an impossible command like this one: "Jump up and down while standing still at the same time." After everyone fails, repeat the pattern. Never let the servants win.

Continue to play until it becomes evident that the servants will never win. Then stop the game and discuss the following questions:

- How did you feel about being a slave?
- When you realized you could never gain freedom, how did you feel?

Searching the Word. Have students read Romans 6:12-14. Then say, "This Bible passage tells us to not be servants of sin. A servant of sin is a person whose thoughts and actions are controlled by sin."

- How is being a servant to sin like being a servant in the game we just played? (You can't escape sin on your own. You can become a slave to sin. Sin isn't fair.)

Now list some sins on a marker board. Have students discuss how these can become habits that control a person's life. (Lying—you tell one lie to cover another. Drinking—it can cause a person to lose self-control. Drugs—people become addicted. Bad TV habits or questionable websites—one's mind becomes polluted.)

Have someone read Romans 6:23. Then say that the ultimate cost of sin is spiritual death. "Sin will cheat us out of everything that is important. Everyone is either following after sin or God. We are the servants of whom we obey, says Romans 6:16-18."

Now read the lesson's key verse, James 4:7. Say, "The Bible tells us God can and wants to set us free from sin habits. We can't do it by ourselves."

- James 4:7 tells us to submit to God. What does that mean?
- James 4:7 also says to resist the devil and he will leave. How can you resist the devil?

"God wants us to offer ourselves to Him to do what is right. When we do that, He will give us strength to not fall into sin habits. We must decide to follow what God wants and not give in to sin."

Applying the Word. Provide markers and paper. Have the preteens draw pictures of themselves breaking any "chains of sin" in their lives. Beside the pictures, have the kids write down how they will submit to God and how they will resist the devil. When they are done, ask them to explain their work.

Acting on the Word. Challenge students to pray about any sinful habits in their lives. Urge them to repent, give themselves to God, and ask for strength to resist sin.

Talking Rocks

The goal of this lesson is to help preteens express their praise to God.

Seeing the Need. "You have probably seen movies or TV shows or video games where pigs, toasters, cars, or even trees could talk. Well, I want you to draw a picture of something that cannot speak. Then draw a speech balloon coming from the object. Think up something for your object to say and write those words in the balloon. It can be funny or serious."

Give the group paper and pencils. Encourage them to be creative. Have all the kids show what they drew.

"Would you like it if things like pencils, flowers, and desks could talk? Why or why not?" Encourage students to respond.

Searching the Word. "It seems far-fetched to think of a pencil or a desk talking. Yet, Jesus said rocks would 'cry out' if a certain thing were to happen."

Have the kids read Luke 19:35-40. "What could cause the rocks to cry out?" (If the people kept quiet and did not praise Jesus.)

"Why do you think Jesus told the Pharisees that if the people were quiet, the rocks would cry out?" (Because it is important and necessary to praise God.)

"Why do you think the Pharisees didn't want the people praising Jesus?" (They were jealous. Praising Jesus was saying Jesus is God, and the Pharisees didn't believe He was God.)

"Verse 37 says the people praised Jesus for the miracles that they had seen Him do. What are some things God has done for you that you can praise Him for?" List their answers on a marker board or chalkboard.

"What are some ways in which we can praise God?" (Tell Him we love Him, tell others about what He has done, sing, lift our hands, write out our praise, illustrate our feelings through dance or art)

Point out that waving palm branches (John 12:13), shouting praises to Jesus, and placing cloaks in His path were ways the people expressed praise on the day we now call "Palm Sunday." The two disciples who got the donkey on which Jesus rode (Luke 19:29-34) were expressing praise by obeying Jesus' command.

Applying the Word. Which of these three best fits you?

- It is easy for me to praise God.

- I feel awkward praising God.
- I usually don't think about praising God.

"Why do you think it is hard for some people to praise God?" (They feel embarrassed, they think it's not cool, they don't understand its importance, or they don't know how.)

"What could you say to encourage someone to praise God?" (God wants us to praise Him; you'll feel better if you praise Him; don't worry about what others think; the more you do it, the easier it becomes.)

Have the preteens choose one or more of the following response activities:

1. Work together in pairs to write a poem of praise.
2. Write a letter of praise to God. Be sure to thank God for specific times He has helped you.
3. Design stickers that will remind you to praise God. Put the stickers on your bathroom mirror, school locker, and anyplace else where you will be reminded to take time to praise God every day.
4. Name 26 things for which you can praise God. Use each letter of the alphabet as a starter (such as A=adults, B=bananas, and so on).
5. Give a short testimony. Begin by saying, "I praise God because He . . . " or "Something that is special to me about God is . . ."
6. Create a praise rap or cheer for the Lord.
7. Put your praise to music through creative movement.

Acting on the Word. As you hold a rock in your hand, ask, "You're not going to let a rock take your place in praising God, are you?"

Have the students take turns saying sentence prayers in which they praise God.

Conclude with a prayer (1) asking for forgiveness for the many times we have forgotten to praise God and (2) committing to praise God each day.

Losing Teeth and Finding God

Wanda Brett

Can it be done? Can you teach God's Word to those gum-chewing, media-smart, one-more-tooth-missing, energy-efficient kids in first, second, and third grade? Holding their attention is difficult—keeping it is next to impossible.

Today's six- to nine-year-olds are being raised on high-tech toys and entertainment. How can you teach them to value a book that is thousands of years old? Is it possible to make the Bible come to life for these students?

The answer is an overwhelming yes. There are many avenues available to the creative teacher. God's Word lends itself to a variety of presentation methods.

In this chapter, we will first explore a variety of ways to creatively teach God's Word to young students. Next, we will look at an issue that is vital to them—finding security. Finally, I've included a sample teaching unit on an important topic—sanctification.

Tremendous Teaching Techniques

The Bible Box

My favorite method is securing a refrigerator box and painting it to make it look like a life-sized replica of a Bible, complete with pages and bookmark. When I tell the story of Noah, for instance, I have someone inside the box waiting on a cue. At the appropriate time, Noah emerges from the pages of our cardboard Bible. (Throwing in some dry ice for dramatic effect isn't bad either.)

Dramatized Stories

Our community always does a living Nativity and each year we add another scene to the Nativity. The children take turns dressing up as Mary and Joseph, angels and shepherds. The story comes to life as the children participate in the event. You can do this with the Resurrection story as well.

When we told the story of David and Goliath, we asked a painter friend to bring stilts and wear them as a life-size giant. We chose a diminutive "David," and provided him with Nerf-style stones to slay the giant on cue.

Puppets Alive

Children enjoy operating puppets or watching a well-done puppet show. It can be as elaborate or as simple as your budget allows.

One of the best puppet shows our class did featured a little lamb who did a quick costume change for each character while the Bible story was being read. One minute he was Daniel (headpiece), the next he was the egotistical king (crown), then an angel (tinsel) . . . and when he turned into a lion (gold yarn), the class cheered.

Hands-on Object Lessons

Have a "feet Sunday" on which you shine a flashlight (labeled "God's Word") on everyone's feet in a semi-darkened room. Your kids will remember that God's Word is a lamp for their feet to follow.

Bring a compass to class and take your students on a short hike. Show them how the compass works and explain to them that God's Word is like a compass: it keeps us from being lost and taking the wrong roads in life.

When telling the story of the Tower of Babel, use several cans of shaving cream. Let students construct a shaving-cream tower, seeing how high they can make it reach. Or bring modeling clay to class and let the children make bricks for the rebuilding of Jerusalem.

Drawing, Cutting, Gluing

When studying Moses, we wrapped butcher paper around the room for a mural on his life. We used construction-paper bulrushes, a glittering crown, bath robes, and a real basket. When Moses received the Ten Commandments, we rolled out six cans of modeling dough, shaped them into a large "stone tablet," and wrote the commandments on it.

A fun lesson was the story of Creation and the giant book we made from poster boards. Each day of creation was a separate page. The students used paint, aluminum foil, and pictures of animals, light, darkness and plant life.

Outdoor Learning

The great outdoors is the ultimate classroom. Unparalleled in beauty and variety, it can be a valuable teaching tool for those active early graders. The challenge is to find ways to use the outdoors in the most effective manner; the secret is to be creative.

Is your lesson about Ruth in the fields of Boaz? Let the outdoors become the field where Ruth gathers the leftover grain.

Is it time to study Jericho? Take your students outdoors and let them shout to the top of their lungs as Jericho falls.

When you learn about Naaman dipping seven times in the Jordan, use a prearranged volunteer wearing old clothes. Have him demonstrate Naaman's faith by dipping in a small wading pool.

If you're studying Luke 19, choose a nearby tree and have an anxious Zacchaeus climb it as the "crowd" (your students) follows Jesus.

The outdoor classroom can provide an exciting way for your creativity to go hand in hand with Biblical truths. Countless Bible stories occurred outdoors. By taking the story back to its origin, it comes to life in a way not possible indoors.

For instance, is your class learning about Rebekah? Assign each child a role in the story: thirsty camels, a worried servant, a young woman and Isaac. Provide a water pitcher, and the story lives!

Perhaps the best part of the outdoors is that it provides a perfect place to do all those messy activities that you hesitate to do inside your classroom. Go ahead—build that 10-foot-long banana split, have the jellybean relay, do the doughnut Frisbee toss! These activities let children get rid of extra energy and help them become more focused during the lesson time.

Memory Verses

"Remember the Sabbath day, to keep it holy." "The Lord is my shepherd; I shall not want."

These two Scripture verses are buried deep in my heart. I learned them when I was a young student in Sunday school. What I find remarkable is that they have stayed with me all these years.

Now that I am teaching early graders, I find my greatest challenge lies within the smallest segment of the lesson—the memory verse! I am constantly looking for new ways to help my kids capitalize on their sharp minds. How can I help them hide God's Word in their hearts and retain it from week to week?

I've written the memory verse on poster board, cut it into jigsaw pieces, and had a contest to see which team could assemble it first. Once I printed each word of the verse on separate Lego blocks and had a construction party.

A class favorite is the chocolate-chip-cookie verse where each child shapes a letter out of cookie dough. We bake it and literally feed the Word to our students! Kids also love decorating a memory-verse confection. Bake a cake and have the class write the verse in icing letters (then take the cake to a shut-in).

My students enjoy dressing up in trench coats and sunglasses and decoding secret messages that are memory verses with missing letters and phrases. I find it helpful to combine craft time and the Scripture verse by making craft projects like Bible verse bookmarks or "scripture quilts" from construction-paper pieces.

My most versatile tool is the Bible neighborhood. I draw a marker-board house, street and street sign. I ask the students, "What street is our memory verse living on?" "John Street," they reply as I fill in the sign. "What is the house address?" "3:16," they shout as I write it in. "And what is the foundation for this house?" "The words of Jesus," they answer as I write the verse on the house's foundation.

Make maximum use of your students' energy by challenging them to hide God's Word in their heart. Your efforts will last a lifetime. I know. "I have hidden your word in my heart that I might not sin against you" (Ps. 119:11).

Beeps and Buzzes

As a primary teacher, today's technology could be threatening. Your students may have spent their Saturday afternoon downloading favorite songs. Before coming to church, perhaps they sent a text message to a friend. And since you saw them last week, who knows how many video games they have played?

Now it's Sunday morning and they come into your classroom. What are their expectations? Will they listen to the gospel presentation in simple terms? Can they appreciate the Word if it doesn't beep, buzz, or blow up?

How can we as teachers reach the media-soaked child for Christ? Shall we do it in sound bites? With one-minute commercials? Maybe! There's no getting around it—we must recognize that a cultural revolution has taken place. The manner in which information is presented is radically changing. Our classrooms must reflect this revolution and acknowledge it at least some of the time.

Should we depend on movies and tablets to do our teaching for us? No! But we should recognize there are some wonderful electronic tools out there and use them to help us present the gospel message in a contemporary fashion. A key to dealing with media-saturated students is to enter their world and use their tools to communicate our message. We should use creative steps to plug our students into the Word—literally! We can use tools like laptop computers, smart phones, and multimedia projectors.

As teachers we have a mandate to deliver the message of God's love. We must use every means available to help our early graders learn and remember the Word. Our job is to help our students hide God's Word in their hearts and hold it in their hands. Any tool that we can use to help our students develop godly character and holy hearts is worth the time and effort that it takes.

Secure in His Loving Hand

The single most valuable lesson we can teach wigglesome and gigglesome primaries is that God loves them with an everlasting, unconditional love.

However, unlike the truth of God's creation of trees and flowers, the lesson of divine love is not one they can touch or see. So how can we make it real to them?

Teach It With Puppets or Drama

One character decides to buy God's love, while another tries to earn it by being very good. Another character says he is so great that God will love him best, while a fourth feels like God will never love him. You can create a delightful lesson as the children assure the characters that God loves each of them the same, just as they are.

Say It With Diamonds

Show students a diamond wedding ring. Explain that when two people get married they give each other rings as a sign of their love.

Next, cut out diamond shapes from construction paper and give each child seven of them. On each diamond the kids should write, "God loves ME!" Encourage them to carry one each day this week to remind them of God's love.

Give It Away

Prepare a "just because" present for each student. These gifts can be inexpensive items, such as bookmarks, brownies or small toys. Wrap the gifts.

In class tell the children, "I am giving you this present just because I love you. You did not do anything special. It is not your birthday. I am giving you this present *just because*."

Explain that God loves them "just because" He does. Help them understand God's love is not something they can earn or buy. It is given to them because God chooses to do so.

Show It With a Store

Turn your class into a store. Bring in household items and place a price tag on each one. Give students play money and let them "shop." (The children should know the items really belong to you and that this is just a game . . . unless you wish to give them the items.)

When the shopping is done, show them a box that has GOD'S LOVE written on it with glitter paint. Inside the box are cardboard cutouts of little presents, with a hole punched in the top of each one. Colorful yarn is strung through the hole. The price tag on each present should read FREE. Have the children open the box and see that God's love is a gift freely given. Each child leaves with a present to hang on their bedroom door.

Make It With a Mural

Your kids will love making a large mural that wraps around your room. In huge letters write "God's Love Is . . . ", and then let the children paint and draw their own expressions of God's love. God's love will be parents, friends, dogs, cats, church, and maybe even chocolate ice cream.

Flesh It Out

The best way to build little lives on the cornerstone of God's unchanging, unconditional love is for us to love primaries as God does—without reservation.

Sample Teaching Unit: Hands, Hearts, and Houses

Begin now teaching your kids the basic building blocks for the Christian life, starting with salvation. Once they have accepted Christ, they are ready to begin learning how to live for Him. Sanctification is one of the next steps.

Holy Hands and Hearts

Sanctification is a long word that translates easily into "holy hands and holy hearts." Let the children dip their hands into paint and press the outline onto an old T-shirt from home. Emphasize that each day when they wake up, it is important to ask Jesus to guide their hands—their actions.

Purchase small wooden hearts and let the children decorate them for key chains or book bags. Each time they look at their heart they will be reminded to pray that the Lord will keep their hearts pure.

A Holy House

A high-energy unit on sanctification continues when your primaries decorate a cardboard house. (Two refrigerator boxes joined together are great for this. You'll need to cut out a door.)

Have students paint, hang curtains, lay carpet scraps, and decorate the house with markers. Add simple furnishings.

Now teach them the message of 1 Corinthians 6:19—their body is the house of the Holy Spirit. Say, "When we receive forgiveness for our sins, Jesus cleans us up and the Holy Spirit comes to live inside. We are as beautiful as a brand-new house."

Begin the next class session by having your children discuss the following questions: "How many of you have to clean up your room or take out the trash?" "What would happen if no one cleaned up your house for several weeks?"

Then have students mess up the cardboard house. Give one volunteer a cup of dirt to sprinkle on the carpet, have another volunteer knock over the chairs, let someone else dirty the walls, and so on.

Explain that if we don't help take care of our body house every day, it will get messed up by sin. "If we say bad words, it is like turning over chairs. If we do unkind things, it is like pouring dirt on clean carpet. Every day we need to ask Jesus to help us keep our lives clean. This is called holy living. When we have holy hands and holy hearts, we are a clean house."

Let the children know that if they disobey God's Word by telling a lie, cheating on a test, or committing another wrong, the Holy Spirit will sweep up the disobedience . . . if they let Him. He will help them clean house so they can live with holy hearts and holy hands.

Bring out a vacuum cleaner and some cleaning supplies. Have the children help you clean the house. Then pray together, asking the Holy Spirit to help your children live obedient lives.

Celebrate a job well done with cookies! Your kids are on their way to a strong foundation for their faith.

Loving and Leading Preschoolers

Pamela Coker Browning

So you teach preschoolers! Aren't they cute and lovable? Don't they renew your faith in humanity with their honesty and willingness to forgive? And I suppose you have noticed that it's not easy to get them to sit still for the entire class period, right? As someone says, such a task is like trying to "nail Jell-O to the wall."

Different people explain the activeness of preschoolers in different ways. Child-development specialists explain it in terms of "short attention spans" and "lack of development of motor control." Parents and teachers describe it in terms of "wiggly bundles of insurmountable, uncontrollable energy." But, for whatever reason, it's the way our Maker chose to create young children.

It is vital that as a teacher or parent you realize it is simply the way preschoolers are. Trite as that may sound, it helps to remind ourselves God knew what He was doing when He designed the master plan for human development. Preschoolers don't have secret meetings to plot how to drive their parents and teachers insane. The energy that sends them off in different directions every 15 seconds is as much a part of their nature as the vivacious smiles and innumerable hugs.

I would suspect that right about now you are saying to yourself, "But you don't know Michael. I have never seen a kid as wild and cantankerous as he is. Just last week he . . . "

Of course, you are right. I don't know that special little one who causes you to stay awake on Saturday night, fervently praying that you will awaken Sunday morning with some plague and have an excuse to stay home. But I can assure you that our heavenly Father knows and loves Michael just as He knows and loves you. You are both made in His image; and His love, understanding and forgiveness has no bounds.

So, next Sunday when Michael is on the verge of driving you to distraction, do this: Stop, look up to the Father, and silently pray, "Thank You, Lord, for creating Michael in Your image. Thank You for loving both of us and for forgiving my impatience." If anyone can help, it is He.

This chapter on ministry to preschoolers zeros in on four areas: their energy level, their level of understanding, their level of worth, and their faith level.

Their Energy Level—Making It Work for You

A few years ago I came upon my pastor's wife observing a group of small children who were acting just as one would expect them to act: running around in circles screaming at the top of their lungs. She shook her head and said, "It's a shame that youth is wasted on children. I could really put that energy to good use!"

Don't we all at times long for the vigor exhibited by those little ones who seem to have no better use for it than to "waste it"?

I, too, often wonder why God chose to design children to have four times more stamina than the adults in their lives. I have cause to wonder about it in raising my own children when they are still going strong long after my bedtime.

But I have a more pressing need to ponder the matter as I attempt to teach a preschool class some sublime biblical truth such as "Obey your mother and father." Why won't they just sit still and listen? After all, I pray about my lesson and prepare fun and exciting activities for the kids. Why doesn't it work the way I want it to work?

I wish I knew. What I do know is that teachers of young children must develop methods of working with their energy rather than against it (unless you enjoy going home frustrated and depressed every Sunday).

Even though I cannot tell you how to control the energy level of your students, I do have three suggestions to help you deal with it.

1. *Divide your lesson into very short segments.* Change activities at least every 10 to 15 minutes. If this is still too long, cut back. If your particular group can handle longer periods of time, go for it.

2. *Alternate quiet, sit-still-type activities with on-the-move activities.* For instance, move from prayer time to an action song to a story to a handcraft.

3. *Tell the children at the beginning of each activity what they will be doing and what you expect of them.* For example, you might say, "It's time

for our story now. During story time I would like to see everyone sitting quietly and looking at the pictures. Are we ready?"

Follow these directions by responding positively to those who react quickly. You could say, "Very nice, Ty and Sara. Thank you for sitting quietly and getting ready to listen." Or you might encourage more children to follow your directions by saying, "Amber is ready. She is looking at our picture board and sitting quietly. Thank you, Amber."

This illustrates a classroom management technique I learned early in my career as an elementary teacher, and I am still amazed at how many children will then pop up straight in their seats and bug their eyes out at the picture board. They want the teacher to tell them that he/she likes the way they are sitting quietly and looking at the picture, too. It doesn't work with every child, but it works with enough to make it well worth the effort. Just don't forget to acknowledge each one with a "thank you" or a "very nice" as soon as they comply with your request.

One last caution: Don't take so long bragging on each child that Tyler has since grown tired of sitting and looking and is off to new adventurers in Sunday School Land!

Their Understanding Level— Teaching When They Aren't Comprehending

Young children do not, actually cannot, think like adults or even older children. The term used to describe this phenomenon is *egocentric*, which, simply put, means "self-centered."

The intent is not to label all young children as selfish but rather to point out that they have had very limited experiences and thereby are limited in their thinking. Also, they have not yet developed the capability of reasoning through something that they have not themselves seen or experienced.

Not a Waste of Time

I can relate the notion of egocentricity to an experience during my days as a schoolteacher. When I would try to explain the significance of Columbus Day to my kindergartners, they simply could not understand. First of all, they had only been on this earth for five years, so there was really no hope of their grasping when 1492 was. Second, most of them had traveled no farther than Grandma's house, so relating to a country thousands of miles away was just expecting too much. Lastly, home is usually a very nice place to a 5-year-old, so why would someone like this Columbus guy want to leave it?

Year after year, I trudged on attempting to explain why we were making ships out of milk cartons, knowing quite well that they were not grasping the purpose. While they might remember the story I was telling them, that was all it was to them—simply a story. However, I felt the story was worth telling. I hoped that if they remembered the story, its significance would become clear to them as well at some point in time.

Now what does any of this have to do with your teaching? Early childhood experts would reason that trying to teach young ones Biblical concepts such as what God is like, what sin is, and what Jesus did for us is a waste of time due to the abstract nature of such teachings. But just like telling the story of Columbus in a memorable way was worth it because later the children would remember the story and grasp its significance, so is it worth teaching your students what God is like, what sin is, and how Jesus gave His life for them.

They will not fully understand these things now, but you can hope and pray that when your students reach the age of understanding, they will remember your teaching and that its meaning will take root in their hearts and minds.

Surprising Insight

In the meantime, you will be amazed at the understanding preschoolers sometimes display. For instance, Kelsy was fascinated with a picture of the empty tomb in her kindergarten Sunday school paper. "Why is it empty, Daddy?" she asked. "Where did He go?"

Her dad kept referring to the picture as he told her the story of how much Jesus loved her. When he finished, she sat quietly, looking at the tomb.

"Daddy," she said, "I need to pray to Jesus right now."

Then there was four-year-old Andrew, who was watching a Sunday school drama on the crucifixion. "Why do they want to hurt Jesus?" he asked as the cross was pulled down the aisle.

"Because they don't understand," his mom said.

He shook his little head. "Well, they weren't listening."

What to Teach

Here are some foundational truths preschoolers should come to understand in preparation for a life with God. These truths need to be taught both by word and by action, by parents as well as by those who minister to children at church.

GOD

- He is the Creator.
- He takes care of us.
- He is always with us.
- We worship Him by singing, giving thanks, and obeying Him.

JESUS
- Jesus is God's Son.
- Jesus grew up. He was a baby, a boy, a teenager, and then a man.
- Jesus helped others.
- Jesus loved children.
- We can love and worship Jesus.
- Jesus died on the cross and came back to life.
- Jesus is preparing a home for us in heaven.

SELF
- God made me.
- God loves me.
- I am special.

OTHERS
- Adults care for me.
- God gives me friends.
- I should be kind to others.
- I should love my family.

PRAYER
- God hears my prayers.
- I can pray anytime and anywhere.
- I can talk to God about anything.
- I should give God thanks every day.

BIBLE
- The Bible is a special book about God.
- The Bible is true.
- The Bible tells me what to do.
- The Bible has exciting stories.
- I should take care of my Bible.

CHURCH
- The church is a place where I learn about God.
- The church is a place to worship God.
- The church is a place where I have friends.

Their Level of Worth—Helping Them Discover It

In a highly competitive, fast-paced world, it is often difficult for small children to find that sense of worth that is so important to their well-being. But they need to know they are valued not only by the adults in their lives, but by God as well. We must teach them that their heavenly Father always cares and they are very special to Him.

Jesus said, "Are not two sparrows sold for a penny? Yet not one of them will fall to the ground apart from the will of your Father. And even the very hairs of your head are all numbered: So don't be afraid; you are worth more than many sparrows" (Matt. 10:29-31).

This passage powerfully communicates that the One who has complete charge over this universe is also so devoted to us that He has counted the hairs on each head. What reassurance that He who loves us so much is in control of every situation! Indeed there is no need for children to fear.

This passage can be easily adapted into an object lesson. After all, that was exactly how the Master Teacher used it. With older preschool children, you could begin by asking them to count the hairs on their head. When they give up in frustration, explain that God cares for them so much that He has the hairs on each head already calculated.

With younger children, you could point to a flock of birds outside the classroom window or show the children a picture of some ordinary birds. Then say, "God cares for these birds so much that not even one of them falls to the ground without His seeing it, and He cares for children much, much more."

Another approach is to hold up a penny and ask the children what they could buy with it. After it has been established that a penny has negligible worth, explain that in the time Jesus lived on the earth, sparrows were so inexpensive that a person could buy two of them for a penny. Yet God cares so much for such a worthless bird that He knows when one falls, and He cares for us more than He cares for many sparrows.

While an object lesson is a great way to introduce preschoolers to the concept of their value to God, it is a message that needs to be repeated frequently. After all, young children sometimes face situations in which they feel unloved and worthless. They need frequent reminders that our God values us above all His creation.

So, be on the lookout for teachable moments you can seize to remind children of God's care. When the children notice a bird on the church grounds, when they discover a penny lying on the floor, or when they get a haircut, you can remind them of the lesson they learned about how valuable they are to God.

Their Level of Faith—Teaching Us to Trust

Our prayers are like seeds. We plant (and we pray) with the hope that our efforts will bring forth a harvest.

However, what we so often do—because we lack the faith to leave our need with the Lord—is continually dig up the seed to see if it has sprouted roots. Obviously, a plant cannot thrive under such abuse, and our prayers are not likely to either.

Romans 12:3 says God has dealt to each one a measure of faith. When we as adults doubt this truth, we can be reminded of the faith we were once dealt by looking at young children.

When preschoolers are told that all they must do is pray and God will hear and answer, by faith they take that promise to heart and begin to act on it. What is more, once they pray for a need—be it a skinned knee, a grandfather's illness, or a sick puppy—they tend to leave it there. They don't think of questioning whether or not their prayers will be answered.

This is one area in which adults can learn more from children than children can learn from adults. Our job as teachers and parents is to nurture such faith rather than dissuade it with our doubts.

Jesus taught in Matthew 17:20 that if we have faith as a mustard seed, we can say to a mountain "move from here to there" and it will move. Unfortunately, most adults would not dare to speak to the smallest of mountains, but I think a 5-year-old would. Furthermore, the child would believe that the mountain indeed would move.

But, you say, what if it does not move—what if God does not say yes to the child's prayer? What will you say to that child? That is, of course, a valid concern; but there is, perhaps, a more critical consideration: What if the mountain does move?

If we feel we must protect a child from disappointment, or even disillusionment, to the point of distracting the child's attention away from that "impossible" prayer, we will never know if the mountain would have moved or not.

We do not want our skepticism to hinder a child's exercise of faith. Instead, we need to heed the Master's bidding to "become like little children" (Matt. 18:3) and exercise our measure of faith along with that of the child.

Other Gifts

In addition to their great faith, there are at least four other gifts preschoolers bring to the church:

Hope for the Future. The church with no small children is a church without a future. But when parents bring their little ones to church, they are making a statement about the importance of the church to the upbringing of their children, and they are saying they want the church to have a future.

The Joy of Community. The unbridled love that small children give members of the church inspires us to be a true community of believers. The four-year-old who points across the aisle and shouts, "There's my teacher!" . . . The two-year-old who holds out his arms to be held by someone he or she hardly knows. . . . The three-year-old who escapes from his pew and runs up the aisle to sit with his mother in the choir loft.

An Example of Humility. The humble nature of children teaches us how we must approach the Almighty God. Jesus said, "Whoever humbles himself like this child is the greatest in the kingdom of heaven" (Matt. 18:4).

An Opportunity for Blessing. Jesus promises His blessing upon those who receive children in His name: "Whoever welcomes a little child . . . in my name welcomes me" (v. 5).

Burps, Diapers, and Joy: Baby Ministry

Cheryl Bridges Johns

At the moment of birth, infants are whole persons. As whole persons they possess everything necessary to be human. This means they are spiritual beings who are seeking to commune with their Creator. Just how do they commune with God? How do they come to know Him?

The basic building blocks of a relationship with God are constructed through early relationships. In the eyes of the parent who mirrors warmth, pride and acceptance, the child comes to understand that there is a God who always keeps him or her in His eye and who offers unconditional love and acceptance.

By receiving consistent care of basic needs within a loving environment, children come to understand that God cares for them and provides for their needs. Within the secure environment of established boundaries, young children come to understand that God has established order for their own well-being.

It is an awesome responsibility to represent God to another human being. But this is what adults are called to do as stewards of the gift of life. If we bless our children, they will come to understand a God who blesses them. If we curse our children, shattering their fragile egos with harsh criticism, they will fear approaching a harsh, demanding God. If we ignore our children, failing to mirror a healthy self-identity, they will have difficulty grasping the existence of a personal God who desires relationship with them.

We are blessed with children, and this blessing comes with heavy responsibilities. We are to nurture our children so that they too will come to know God in an intimate and covenantal manner. If we did not exist in a sinful world, this process would be easy; but sin seeks to destroy our children. We are always at war for the souls of our children. Until they are strong enough to be full warriors in this warfare, we are to fight for them. Prayer, therefore, is a critical element. We should begin praying for our children before they are born and cover them with prayer on a daily basis.

The Church's Care for Parents

The chief responsibility of the church for infants is to enfold their parents into the church as a community that provides support for them as the primary caretakers. The support of parents should include informed premarital counseling, prenatal counseling, extensive care during the postnatal period, and corporate acts of celebration and dedication of the child.

Premarital Counseling

The care of children begins with the creation of loving families. Pastors have a responsibility to make certain that couples planning to be married are prepared to create a lasting, stable, and godly environment in which to raise a family. All too often couples are married without adequate instruction on the Biblical basis for marriage and family. Premarital counseling should include a study of Christian parenting.

The couple must understand that children are a gift from God and that a covenant of love and care for children is explicitly contained in the covenant of marriage.

Prenatal Counseling

The church has a special responsibility to see that a young couple is spiritually and emotionally prepared for the birth of their first child. Where possible this instruction should take place in the home; however, "expectant parent classes" during midweek services may be a viable alternative to a home environment. Such a class should be directed by the pastor or someone appointed by the church who understands the unique needs of this peak event in a couple's life. Lessons should be aimed at renewing the couple's wedding vows, preparing them for the unfolding transitions in lifestyle, training them in the care of a newborn, planning for the child's enfoldment into the life of the church, and preparing for the spiritual nurture of the child.

Extensive Care

The birth of a child—especially the first child—is a critical event in the life of a mother and father. A pastoral figure should be present within hours of the birth when possible. At moments like these the pastor is the visible representative of God for most Christians. He or she should consciously bring his or her presence into the situation. A warm, personal prayer is always appropriate.

Support Group for New Parents

In an age when extended families living close together are the exception, there is a great need for support systems for new parents. Many young couples (and single mothers) face parenthood with little preparation and are filled with insecurities. The church, therefore, should offer support/enrichment groups which speak to this real need. These groups, which are usually designed to meet monthly or biweekly, offer times to share with other parents and to learn about child development and parenting.

Between the actual meetings, parents feel secure by knowing they have a support system to call on when in need of advice. New-parent groups usually form a unit of care in which there is deep bonding as parents experience together the exciting and precarious journey of new parenthood.

Acts of Enfoldment

Two ceremonies of enfoldment may be especially helpful in renewing the congregation's covenant to nurture its children: a birth celebration and baby dedication.

Birth Celebration

Birth is a time to celebrate the gift of life which has been given not only to the parents but to the whole congregation. This gift should be welcomed with joy and with a commitment to be faithful stewards. A birth celebration is an appropriate means for expressing both joy and commitment. These celebrations are more than baby showers—they are opportunities for the whole congregation to welcome its newest addition. The format of birth celebrations is flexible but should include the following:

1. A time to give blessings to the new baby and his/her parents. These blessings should be written and expressed orally. They are simple expressions of church members' hopes, desires and commitments to the baby. For example, a blessing may read as follows: "It is my desire that as you grow you will come to know and love God. May you come to be aware of His presence and may His hand guide your life. I offer to you my prayers and my time."

   Each person's blessing should be read to the parents, and then compiled in the form of a scrapbook which may be labeled "A book of blessings for . . . ." This scrapbook should be given to the parents, who in turn, keep the book for the child. Then the newborn is blessed by his or her parents, who add their blessings to the scrapbook. As the child grows, the scrapbook of blessings becomes a visible reminder that he or she is loved and blessed.

2. A time to give gifts to the infant. Members of the congregation not only provide written blessings but they also give gifts that are needed for the

infant's care. These gifts are expressions of care and joy and go a long way toward helping a young couple obtain all of the necessary items for their new arrival.

3. A time for prayer for the parents and infant. Birth celebrations should include a time of concerted prayer for God's blessings upon both the infant and the parent.

4. A time of food and fellowship. Birth celebrations need to include refreshments and a time for informal talk. The atmosphere should be warm and relaxed rather than formal.

Birth celebrations recapture the Biblical model of the involvement of the community of faith and the parents with each other and with God as they receive this gift with joy.

Baby Dedication

Baby dedication is an act which acknowledges that children are not possessions of the parents but that they belong to God. Parents and the local congregation are keepers of a treasure which will one day return to God. Infant dedication is an act of promise and of hope. As an act of promise, it is a time in which the parents and the congregation covenant together in a solemn pledge to faithfully keep and develop their treasure. As an act of hope, infant dedication is a time to place children in the hands of God, who will make for them a hopeful future.

Because infant dedication is a time of covenanting in the presence of God, it should not be taken lightly. It is not a time to "show off" the new baby nor is it a mere formality that is hurried through so "real worship" can occur. Infant dedication is an act of worship which reminds us that God is the giver of life and that all life belongs to Him. Therefore, the ceremony itself should take into consideration the following elements:

1. Commitments on the part of the parents who pledge to raise their child in the nurture and admonition of the Lord.

2. Commitments from the congregation who pledge to be faithful in providing a nurturing and supporting community for the child and his/her parents.

3. A prayer of dedication offered by the pastor which summarizes the commitments and hopes found within the pledges.

Infant dedication can be a holy event in which God's Spirit is acknowledged as the source and the sealer of the covenants made. In our congregations, if every child was viewed as holy unto the Lord and received as such and nurtured as we would precious treasure, then we would find that our children would more readily identify with God and their church as they enter adolescence. While we have no guarantee of their salvation, we must do our best to call them to a life of faithful obedience by our faithfulness to them.

The Church Nursery

A Toddler's Litany

Mommy loves me . . .

Daddy loves me . . .

Sister loves me . . .

Church loves me . . .

Jesus loves me.

—Lauren Thompson

There is no place in the life of the church quite like the nursery! Most would view it as a necessary ministry, but often there are only a few people who are willing to devote their time and energy to the care of infants and toddlers. Consequently, the nursery is quite frequently a source of frustration for pastors, education ministers, and parents.

In an age in which ministry is viewed as a performance, nursery workers are not perceived as legitimate "ministers." However, the church nursery is a vital ministry. It is a place where infants and toddlers have their first experience of "church." Those nursery experiences can help establish a foundation of trust, love, and hope.

To have a good nursery, there are a few essential ingredients. These ingredients provide the proper foundation.

A Stable Environment

In order to establish trust, babies and toddlers need to bond with a few adults who become "anchor points" in what can at times be a frightening and overwhelming world. In the church nursery, a stable environment is created by one or two faithful people who are with the babies every week.

The Proper Ratio of Adults to Infants

Any nursery, no matter how small, should be staffed by two workers. Babies require the lowest worker-to-child ratios: ideally a minimum of one worker for every two infants. Add one worker for every three to four crawlers or four to six walkers.

Nursery ministry requires some one-to-one contact between the nursery workers and infants. Each child needs to be held, hugged, fed, diapered, and played with. Some will need to be rocked, while others will need to be taken to the "potty." Some babies will want an adult to express delight in every activity. An exhausted nursery worker who attempts to manage a room full of infants and toddlers cannot adequately provide an environment conducive to developing within the very young child a sense of security and warmth.

A Clean, Healthy Environment

The room, or rooms, that houses the very young should be the cleanest in the church. Linens should be changed every service, the floors should be washed and disinfected on a regular basis, and toys should be cleaned after each session. The room should not be in a damp, dark basement. There should be a minimum of 20 to 30 square feet of floor space for each child. If possible, the younger babies should be separated from the crawlers and toddlers. Equipment should be sturdy. Avoid old items that may need repair and could cause accidents.

A Congregation Who Owns the Nursery as Ministry

Many congregations want to hire someone from the outside to give care to their infants and toddlers. This is a noncovenantal approach which does not take seriously the responsibility of caring for and bringing God to the gifts of life found within the walls of the nursery.

We need to see the babies and toddlers as precious treasures, deserving the best of our time and resources. They deserve our ministry.

Nursery Ministry Guidelines

Following are guidelines a church can adapt in developing its nursery policies.

Philosophy of Child Care

Our congregation's nursery ministry is dedicated to partnering with parents in their attempt to lay a spiritual foundation in the lives of children that will in God's timing and in God's way (1) lead each child into a saving relationship with God through Jesus Christ and (2) enhance the process of Christian discipleship.

The priority of safety. You have a very serious responsibility. The parents are trusting you to ensure the safety of their children while they are here at church. Always keep your eyes and ears open for safety hazards and potential accidents.

The priority of quality care. Always provide prompt and professional care for the children's physical, emotional, and social needs. Be sensitive to needs according to the developmental levels of the children.

The priority of spirituality. Always take the opportunity to help lay a spiritual foundation in the lives of our youngest children. Jesus' love is taught through your loving attitude, prayerful concern, and smiling face. You are also an extension of the parent's ministry to their little ones.

Nursery Staff

Nursery workers must be properly screened before they are allowed to serve in the nursery.

Nursery staff are identified by the smocks they wear.

Anyone under 16 years of age is not allowed to work or loiter in the nursery.

Check In
1. Greet the parents at the door with a smile.
2. Make sure all the baby's belongings are labeled.
3. Mark the baby attendance roll (Sunday morning and Wednesday night).
4. Note any specific instructions from the parents.

Check Out

When the child is picked up, inform the parent about when the child was fed, changed, and if the child slept.

Allow only the person who brought the child or another authorized individual to pick up the child.

Health Guidelines

If a child exhibits any of these symptoms, he or she should not be allowed in the nursery:

- symptoms of a sore throat in conjunction with fever and swollen glands
- a temperature of 101 degrees or above
- presently being treated for strep throat
- chicken pox
- pin-head sized red dots too numerous to count, prominent over cheeks, chest, and abdomen
- pink eye
- thick green or yellow mucus draining from the nose
- drainage from the ear
- a cough bringing up phlegm
- vomiting within the last 12 hours.

Proper hand-washing is required following contact with any body fluid and includes vigorous washing with fresh warm water and soap for a minimum of 10 seconds.

Getting Ready

The nursery worker should be ready to receive children 15 minutes prior to the beginning of each service.

Spray toys with disinfectant before service.

Pray for the children who will be coming to the nursery.

Put clean sheets on the beds.

Nursery Procedures

There should always be two adults present.

Pray over the children individually.

Keep the baby clean. If his clothes become soiled, change them.

If a child is unhappy and cannot be calmed down within a reasonable amount of time, call in the parent or guardian.

Do not take care of personal business in the nursery.

After Service

Take all sheets off the cribs.

Wash cribs, chest, counters, door, and mirror with disinfectant.

Place garbage bag outside nursery door.

Diapering

1. Check each child every 30 minutes to see if their diaper is either wet or soiled.
2. Check all children just prior to dismissal to make sure no child leaves the room wet or soiled.
3. Have all supplies assembled and ready before you begin. These include diapers and disposable gloves.
4. Never walk away from a child when changing a diaper.
5. Always wash hands with soap and water to sanitize your hands. Use after every diaper change and between caring for different children.
6. Waxed paper should be used as a changing pad for each change. Soiled disposable diapers must be put into a plastic bag and put into the trash can.
7. Do not use powder or ointments unless the parent has advised you to do so.
8. Make diaper-changing pleasant for the child. Avoid showing any distaste. Smile and talk or sing to the child.
9. Place disposable diapers in the trash can. Trash should be emptied into exterior trash receptacle at the end of each session.
10. If diapers are changed on the floor, place the child on a mat or pad, cover the pad with wax paper and change the diaper. After diaper change, clean the mat with a cleaning solution.
11. Babies may be changed in their own bed. Make sure you use wax paper.
12. Record the diaper change on a Nursery Ministry Card (see next page).

Nursery Ministry
Notes to Parents

Child's Name: _____

Today's Date: _____

Today your child:

    ___ was content

    ___ cried when you left but settled quickly

    ___ was fussy

Your child was given a bottle at _____.

Your child's diaper was checked/changed at _____ and was

    ___ wet   ___ soiled   ___ dry

Your child napped for _____ minutes.

Additional comments: _____

_____

_____

If today was your child's first time in the nursery, we welcome you to our ministry.

Building a Lesson Kids Will Love

Wilson Kilgore

Brian, a third grader, described his Sunday school class like this: "The kids just sit there while the teachers talk."

Ask the average child in the children's department of a typical Sunday school to describe their class in one word and you might hear, "Boring!"

How can we as teachers insure that our lessons are not boring? It will take an attitude change, commitment, sacrifice and work to change the atmosphere of our classrooms from "ho-hum" to "wow!"

First, it is time for an attitude check. Do you look forward to Sunday morning? Do you enjoy studying and preparing for each week's lesson? Are you so excited about the Word of God that you can hardly wait to share it with the kids in your class?

If you answer no to any of these questions, you need to pray for the Holy Spirit to change your attitude. Your kids will be no more excited about the lesson than you are. You will never be able to build a lesson kids will love until you are excited about communicating God's truth to your students.

Second, teaching a lesson kids will love requires commitment. There's no place for halfhearted effort in Christian teaching. God called and gifted you to teach. In the words of an old U.S. Army slogan, "Be all that you can be."

The Holy Spirit will help you to change your attitude, but you must renew your commitment.

Third, effective teaching calls for sacrifice. Building a lesson that kids will love, week after week, will cost you. It will cost you the one commodity that is probably most precious to you—time. It takes time to study the Word, pray for your students, experiment with new techniques and methods, and get to know your students.

Fourth, building a lesson kids will love requires work. After all has been said and done, more is usually said than done. Building requires that someone work. Remember, as you build that lesson your kids will love, you are also building kids to love Jesus. Work can be hard, but it is also sweet. Many teachers don't want to take the time or put forth the extra energy needed to make a lesson truly memorable. However, it is the lessons that have the "extra" in them that kids will remember until they are 80 years old!

The FACTS

How do you translate a changed attitude, a renewed commitment, a willingness to sacrifice, and a heart to work into a lesson that your kids can't wait to get to and learn? Good question, huh?

I will use the word FACTS as an acrostic to offer some principles that will help you build lessons kids will love. These principles are **F**un, **A**ctive, **C**reative, **T**esting, and **S**trategic.

Fun

Kids want to have fun. Their lives revolve around play and fun. In fact, play is one of their primary ways of learning.

Make sure your classroom is a fun place to be. Smiles and laughter should be a normal part of your lesson. Sure there is a time to be serious. But the serious times should be sandwiched between times of fun.

Beautify your room. Is your classroom a bright, colorful and cheery place? It ought to be. Paint your walls bright colors. Better yet, get your pastor's permission to have the kids meet you on a Saturday to do the painting. Take down those drab, dusty, and stained pictures that have been hanging in your room for years and put up new, colorful posters—posters which the kids choose from your Christian bookstore.

Plan fun. Plan fun events with your students outside of the classroom. This is a sure way to build relationships with them. (What if the only time Jesus spent time with the disciples was on the Sabbath in the synagogue or Temple?)

Active

God gave children five senses with which to learn. Why then do we do what Brian said in the introduction—"just talk"? Why do we insist on focusing on only one sense—the sense of hearing? Kids learn by impression (hearing, seeing, touching), and they learn by expression (thinking, doing, speaking). Every children's class should include both impression and expression.

How did you learn how to read—by hearing about it or doing it? How did you learn how to drive—by reading the driver's manual or by getting behind the wheel? How will your kids learn how to witness for Christ—by hearing about it or by practicing it?

Children were not designed by their Creator to sit still for more than a few minutes at a time. Certainly not for a whole hour! So why do we expend so much time and energy trying to get them to sit still and listen? That's like telling water to be dry. Sure there will be times for stillness and listening, but those moments should follow on the heels of an active time of learning.

I challenge you to plan your lessons in ways that require your students to get the workbooks and pencils out of their hands and their bodies out of their chairs. Kids were designed by the Creator to be active, so they will be active! They will be active on their terms or they will be active on your terms.

Creative

You develop a creative lesson by being creative! But you say, "I'm not a creative person."

Sure you are! You may have to pray and work to bring it out, but you are creative. How do I know this? Because the Bible says you were made in the image of God, and He is a creative God.

The dictionary defines *creating* as "being productive" or "making something." You are called to make disciples of the kids in your class. Also implied in the word *creative* is the idea of something being original rather than an imitation. The worst teaching method you can use is the one you use all the time. Being creative means to be willing to try something new or to do something in a new way. The seven last words of any dying class are, "We've never done it that way before."

Try some of these effective but under-used methods: role-play, games, simulation activities, mini-dramas, finger painting, and building a model. However, you don't have to "build" something to be creative in teaching. Keep an eye out for props that will help you get your lesson across. Sometimes just bringing in a big object that relates to the story can grab the class's attention.

How about these ideas?
- For a lesson on God's provision of manna in the wilderness, let the kids prepare popcorn. (Be ready for visitors to your class from all over the church!)
- For a lesson on Jesus calling His disciples to be fishers of men, put water in a wading pool in your classroom and let the kids go "fishing."

- When talking about "holding onto Jesus," bring in a pair of roller skates. Ask a child who has never skated to try to skate. He or she will automatically want to hold on to something while they try to skate.

- Ask around to see if anyone in your church has a decorative sword. This works beautifully in demonstrating the "sword of the Spirit".

- Crazy ways we've taught lessons: A motorcycle was driven into the service, Sprite was poured on a child's head to represent the "Spirit" being poured out on all flesh (every child left with a Sprite drink that day), a three-legged dog was brought in, hair was spray-painted green, four-foot lips were hung from the ceiling, a leaf blower shot toilet paper off its roll in less than 60 seconds. These ideas all seem crazy, but each one was used to teach a specific lesson, and I can guarantee you the children remember it.

Testing

This is often a missing ingredient in Christian teaching. Admittedly, it carries a negative connotation because of school experiences. (Talk about testing and most of us break into a cold sweat!) But how do you know you have effectively taught if you don't provide a means of testing your students?

Don't get nervous—I am not suggesting that you start making up multiple-choice or essay exams to give to your students. Instead, under the leadership of the Holy Spirit, find opportunities to put your students in real-life situations that challenge them to apply the Biblical principles you are teaching them. In other words, give them the opportunity to put their faith in action. Here are examples:

- When teaching about witnessing, take students to a walking trail and hand out bottled water labeled "Jesus loves you."

- When teaching about loving your neighbor, have your group visit a nursing home and sing to the elderly there.

- When teaching about God's provision, have your class help feed the hungry by serving in a soup kitchen or collecting food.

These examples may not seem like tests, but they are. You will do your kids a favor by arranging for testing. As they successfully "pass" the tests of faith in action, they will gain confidence and grow spiritually.

Strategic

To be successful, every lesson must have a plan or strategy. The following three-step approach can work for every lesson: (1) begin with the life situation of the children, (2) move to the truth of God's Word, and (3) challenge the children to apply that truth to their lives.

First, your lesson must be relevant to your kids. If you begin where they live, you will immediately have their attention. To do this you will need to know three things.

1. The general age-level characteristics of the children you are teaching.
2. The specific life situations of the kids in your class (which you will discover by talking with the kids and their parents and by spending time with them outside the class).
3. The effects of our contemporary society on kids. Kids today live in a new world. Things are not the same as when you were a child. Do you know which TV programs they are watching? Which video games they are playing? What they are being taught in our secularized schools?

Second, move them from their life situation to the relevant principles of God's Word. What does the Bible say to them in their specific situations? It is critical that you get your kids interacting with the Word in enjoyable, active, and creative ways. Use variety; don't bore them!

There is nothing more exciting than God's Word. Use methods most appropriate for your kids and their needs—not just the ones you are comfortable with.

Third, apply the lesson. Truth not applied and not practiced is of little use to your kids. Indeed this may be the most important part of your strategy of building lessons kids will love. Only when they realize God's Word is relevant to their situation and then apply it to their daily life will you be able to say you have really taught! This is where testing comes into play for *you*: Are kids changing their attitudes, behavior, and choices based on truths you are teaching?

It's Time to Build

In order to build lessons kids will love, you will have to pray, prepare, study, and work hard. But it is worth it!

How about starting this week as a member of God's construction crew? Begin building lessons kids will love.

Reflect on this poem written by Thomas Curtis Clarke:

A teacher built a temple

With loving and infinite care,

Planning each arch with patience,

Laying each stone with prayer.

None praised her unceasing efforts,

None knew of her wondrous plan,

For the temple the teacher built,

Was unseen by the eyes of men.

Scripture Memory: It Can Be Done

Lynn Miller

As leaders of the emerging generation, we all know the important role Scripture should play in the lives of our children. You have probably even quoted 2 Timothy 3:16 to your kids: "All scripture is given by inspiration of God, and is profitable for doctrine, for reproof, for correction, for instruction in righteousness, that the man of God may be complete, thoroughly equipped for every good work." Have you also quoted verse 15 to them? It says, "From childhood you have known the Holy Scriptures, which are able to make you wise for salvation through faith which is in Christ Jesus."

"From childhood." Did you catch that? Those who "have known the Holy Scriptures" from childhood are wise to God's salvation and able to have faith in Jesus. It is our job to make the Scriptures "known" to the children we teach.

Scripture memorization isn't impossible for children to accomplish. In fact, Jewish tradition required that all male children memorize and recite the entire first four books of the Old Testament by the age of 13. During our annual Vacation Bible School we pre-select a chapter in the Bible and announce to the children that they will receive a reward if they can recite the entire chapter by the end of the week. There has never been a year when children didn't recite the entire passage, and they learned it in only one week's time. We know it can be done, so the question is, "How?" It is done with planning, creativity and rewards.

Planning

To get children to memorize anything you have to plan your approach. If you want them to learn scriptures through music, you will have to do the time-consuming task of finding the appropriate song. Showing verses on a big screen requires typing the words into a computer program or copying them from another source. This all takes planning.

Many leaders fail to plan and instead quickly decide on a Scripture memorization method right before they teach their lesson. They pull from whatever they've done in the past or look through their cabinets for whatever props are immediately available. When this is done, the children probably won't learn the Bible verse and thus will fail to obey it. After all, God's Word helps us not to sin. "Your word have I hid in my heart, that I might not sin against you" (Ps. 119:11).

Be intentional when you plan the lesson. Give extra time, not spare time, to figuring out how to get God's Word, which "will by no means pass away" (Matt. 24:35), into the hearts of your students. If, while reading this, you have realized that planning is something you have failed to do properly, stop right now and pray about it:

Father, I know Your Word is important, and it has changed my life. Please forgive me for placing such little emphasis on memorizing it when I teach Your children. I realize that I don't spend enough time planning my lessons. Help me to give Scripture memorization the amount of time and attention needed to make it memorable to the children. Amen.

Creativity

Before teaching a Scripture verse, lead your children in prayer. Teach them to ask God to help them not just know the verse in their head, but also understand it in their heart. Children must realize that simply memorizing scriptures isn't going to save them. However, scriptures that are committed to memory will help to keep them holy. A memorized verse can be used by the Holy Spirit to remind a child how to act during temptation.

Single-Verse Memorization

Let's consider some simple techniques you can use to help a scripture take hold in a child's heart.

1. Use objects that can help children visualize the scripture. Example: Proverbs 12:22 says, "The Lord detests lying lips, but he delights in men who are truthful." Cut out two sets of giant lips from red poster board.

2. Preach the verse. The leader acts like a traditional Pentecostal preacher, preaching the verse line by line. If the leader pounds his fist as he says "no condemnation for those who are in Christ Jesus" (Rom. 8:1), the children pound their fist while repeating those words. If the leader shakes his finger in the air, the children shake their fingers in the air. Use phrases

such as "Again I say" or "Amen and amen" between repeating the verse. Children absolutely love this form of memorization because it is loud and active.

3. Role-play the verse. 1 Samuel 16:7 says, "Man looks on the outward appearance but the Lord looks at the heart." Pin a paper heart that has spots (sin) on it to a child's shirt, and then place a button-up shirt on him. The shirt should cover the heart. Place a sign around a second volunteer's neck that reads "Man." "Man" will look at the first child and give him a "thumbs up." Replace the sign on the second child with one that reads "God." "God" will look at the child, discover the sinful heart, and sadly shake his head. Reverse the situation: use a clean heart, hiding it with a wrinkled and torn shirt. "Man" does not approve this time, but "God" does.

4. Play "take away." Write the scripture on a dry-erase board or individual pieces of paper. After repeating the verse a few times, begin taking away a word at a time. Continue to repeat the verse just as if the words were still visible until all are gone.

5. Teach a character. Have the kids teach the verse to a drama or puppet character. The character says the verse wrong several times. After each try the children repeat the verse correctly, and the character gets closer to saying it correctly. An example is 1 John 1:9. (1) The character says, "If we confess, then we'll get caught and have to do the dishes for a month!" (2) "If we confess our sins, he will beat us with a big fat fish and we won't be able to get the smell out . . . ever!" (3) "If we confess our sins, he is faithful and just and will see to it that we go to after-school detention." (4) "If we confess our sins, he is faithful and just and will forgive us our sins, but won't let us ever watch TV again." (5) "If we confess our sins, he is faithful and just and will forgive us our sins, and will cleanse of all our spaghetti stains." (6) The character recites the verse correctly.

6. Hands-on activities.
    a. Use flashcards.
    b. Make a Scripture verse puzzle.
    c. Do a sword drill (a contest to see who can locate the verse in their Bible the quickest).
    d. Add motions for key words.
    e. Use a different accent or voice tone each time you repeat the verse.
    f. Make a Bible craft.
    g. Create classroom Scripture posters.
    h. Make greeting cards featuring the Bible verse.

i. Time the children to see who can say the verse the quickest from memory.

j. Use symbols to replace key words. (Draw an eye for the word "I"; draw a soda can for the word "can"; and so on.)

Multiple Verse Memorization

To teach larger sections of the Bible, you'll need to use more intense techniques.

Music is an excellent way to remember exact phrases. There are several songs available that have exact Bible verses in the lyrics. However, there aren't any songs available that teach entire passages. To do this yourself, pick out a soundtrack to a familiar song. Have the children help apply the words of a specific passage to the song. Replace the lyrics with your Bible verses, and you are ready to go!

Dividing the passage into smaller sections will make it easier to memorize. Give the children a new portion of the passage each week. Have them build on their knowledge little by little. Each week have them recite what they have already learned and then add the new material. This constantly reinforces what they have already committed to memory.

Writing verses is a good hands-on method. Have a contest to see who can get the material down on paper the quickest. I know firsthand that writing down information helps in memorization. Once in the eighth grade, I planned to cheat on a test. I tried to write all of the answers to the test on an index card, but I ran out of room on the first try and had to rewrite the information, this time in smaller print. Still, I ran out of room and had to rewrite the information again. When it came time to take the test, I never even pulled out the "cheat sheet." I knew all of the answers because I had written and rewritten them. And, yes, I asked God to forgive me for my premeditated sin.

Play board games with the scriptures. Learning the verses allows the players to move around the board. This method takes plenty of preparation because you will have to rewrite the rules of the game to fit your memorization needs. Some games will require you to create new cards or board spaces.

Play outside games like baseball, kickball or yard darts. In darts, the child gets one dart for each section of the passage he or she can recite. In baseball or kickball, the children get up to kick (or bat) by reciting the passage. To make the game more interesting, the fielders can have the option of getting the kicker or batter out if they can recite a specific verse before the runner reaches base.

Create ministry opportunities that will encourage the memorization to be completed by a given date. For example, let them recite the passage in a worship service or discipleship class. This kind of activity can be intimidating for some children, but also very rewarding once they receive the loud applause afterwards!

Hold a "consecutive scripture challenge." This contest can be between just the children or between children and adults. In the adult challenge, the children who have memorized more than one chapter have an advantage because, other than Psalm 23 and the Lord's Prayer, most adults usually only know single verses.

Assign study partners. Encourage the children to have their partner over for a memory/play time. Or, they can spend a few minutes on the phone with their study partner challenging each other to learn the passage.

These are just a few ways to creatively encourage your children to memorize God's Word. If you are not the kind of person who is overflowing with new ways to do ministry, take heart. I'm not either. Most of what I do in ministry comes from someone else's brain power. I listen to other people's ideas and then tweak them to fit my group's needs. I read magazines, talk to other leaders, and chat with professional teachers (you know, those amazing people who spend all day trying to get children to memorize the multiplication tables!). I also pray. If you think you are not creative enough to tackle Scripture memorization, take a minute to pray:

Father, You are the Creator of the universe. You have ultimate creative powers and, in all Your wisdom and humor, You created me. Now You have given me the task of teaching children Your Word. I need Your help here. You understand the children in my group. You know what will grab their interest and motivate them. Please open my eyes to the creative ways I can help them commit Your words to memory. Amen.

Rewards

Our God is big on rewards. To those who follow Him, He promises an eternity with no sorrow, a new home, a new name, and a new body.

Rewards are crucial in motivating children to reach goals. Use them, being sure to always follow through with whatever you promise. Proverbs 25:14 says, "Like clouds and wind without rain is a man who boasts of gifts he does not give."

Rewards can cost as much or as little as you want. There are four categories: free, nearly free, reasonable, and expensive. A good memorization program should have several of the free and nearly free rewards and a few costly rewards. Give children a goal to work towards without losing sight of the real reward: "The ordinances of the Lord are sure and altogether righteous. They are more precious than gold, than much pure gold; they are sweeter than honey, than honey from the comb. By them is your servant warned; in keeping them there is great reward" (Ps. 19:9-11).

Free rewards work best for the interim goals of your program:

*extra play time at the end of class *recognition in worship services *recognition in take-home paper/newsletter/church bulletin *special recital in an adult class *special seating: front row, bean bag, or the teacher's chair *honorary assistant teacher for a younger class *name posted on a bulletin board *leader for the day

Nearly free rewards work well for interim goals as well:

*a card sent to the child's home *small gift item: ball, yo-yo, pencil, sticker, dollar-store toy *soda *homemade goody *candy *certificate *popsicle *kid's meal coupon (these can usually be obtained as a donation)

Reasonably priced rewards work very well for the end goal:

*lunch with the leader/pastor *class party *movie night *new Bible *DVD's *naming rights to a new puppet *pizza delivered just for child *family play date with the leader *gift certificates: super center, fast food, movie theater, book store *child's name printed in local newspaper *T-shirt/ball cap (Note: Some businesses may donate a few of these items if you send a letter stating the reason for the reward.)

Expensive rewards should be reserved for children memorizing very large sections of Scripture:

*Christian concert tickets *free tuition to youth camp *high-dollar gift certificate *chaperoned trip *day pass or season pass to a theme park *limo ride and fancy dinner *musical instrument (Note: Church members may be able to sponsor these kinds of rewards if you do not have a church budget or if your budget cannot support a reward of this caliber. There are organizations that may donate a service if you send a letter stating that the service will be used as a reward. You have not because you ask not!)

Disciplining the Undisciplined Child

Daniel C. Bunce

We've all had them. If you've served in children's ministry for any length of time, you've had those Sundays and Wednesdays that tried every bit of your patience. I "affectionately" call them "McDonald's Sundays"—days when I leave kids church, go back to my office, and think, *I'm going to quit and get a job at McDonald's. I can still go to heaven flipping burgers for a living; that may not be the case if I stay in this ministry!*

More often than not, these days are a result of discipline problems with your kids. You pray and study all week to teach your class or speak your message, only to be constantly interrupted telling kids to sit down, stop talking, quit touching their neighbor . . . and the list of infractions goes on and on.

Discipline can be a sensitive subject, especially when dealing with a collection of parents who have various philosophies and methods of discipline. You have everyone from the mother who thinks her sweet angel can do no wrong, to the father who insists his kids act in a manner that would make the most hardened drill instructor proud.

However, make no mistake—*discipline* is a biblical principle. The word itself comes from the Latin word *disciplina*, meaning "instruction given, teaching, learning, knowledge"—attributes that Jesus Christ exhibited. Hebrews 12:11 tells us, "We do not enjoy being disciplined. It is painful at the time, but later, after we have learned from it, we have peace, because we start living in the right way" (NCV).

It would be naive to think there is one formula for discipline that works in every setting—a method you can take from an article, implement in your ministry, and your problems are solved. As with everything in children's ministry, one size does not fit all. However, there are some key principles, foundations really, for developing a strategy for discipline that will work for you.

Relationships

The saying "They don't care how much you know until they know how much you care" has been attributed to everyone from Teddy Roosevelt to John Maxwell. This statement, however, captures the importance relationships play in a discipline strategy.

Getting to know those you serve lets them know that you care. If kids know you have their best interest at heart, it's easier for them to take correction from you. This is true not only with kids but with their parents also.

Find ways to interact. For example, be out front during check-in and checkout of kids church so you can meet and greet kids and their parents. At the beginning of Sunday school or club, be at the door to say hello, shake hands, and give hugs.

Go to kids' baseball games, soccer matches, school plays, dance recitals, and chorus concerts. Be sure to include all your kids and not just the ones who are the most outgoing and with whom you have the most in common. Give attention to the ones who are the most awkward and introverted. These are often the kids who need that relationship-building the most.

Building relationships with families is especially important with kids whose parents/guardians don't have a connection with your church, such as kids who attend through a bus ministry. It is important to find ways to connect with these families. Visits to kids' homes are a great way to build good relationships with parents and discuss issues regarding their children.

When you talk with parents, you can learn of special needs and challenges their kids might have. For example, a child with a learning disability, ADHD, or autism faces challenges you need to address. Building a relationship with parents allows you to partner with them to provide the best possible environment for their children to receive ministry.

When you build a connection with kids and their families, you are able to make corrections from the position of someone who has taken the time and effort to show just how much you care—with your actions and not just your words.

Expectations and Consequences

We cannot expect children to act a certain manner if we have not clearly defined what we expect of them. Whether you teach a class on Sunday or

Wednesday, or preach a message in kids church, you need to have a clear set of rules for each situation. These rules need to be simple enough for kids to understand and follow, and kids need to be reminded of them each week.

In creating your expectations, consider the routine of your ministry and the physical makeup of children. For example, if Sunday morning includes classroom time before kids church, it will be difficult for a child to sit still for a lengthy period of time in kids church. They have just spent an hour or so sitting in a classroom, so taking time to move and exert some of their energy is imperative. You cannot expect them to simply sit still and listen to your Bible lesson, no matter how well you teach. Beginning with a high-energy song that gets them moving or an active game can help you work with their God-created physiology to avert discipline problems before they occur.

Expectations need to contain consequences—both negative and positive. Consequences need to be as clearly defined as the expectations. Why should a child sit still in class if they know nothing negative will happen if they are non-compliant? Negative consequences should be reasonable and intended to teach and correct, never to embarrass or berate.

Be sure to reinforce positive behavior with positive consequences. It's no coincidence that the single command [from the Ten Commandments] that specifically deals with the parent/child relationship is the only one to have a reward mentioned. Exodus 20:12 says, "Honor your father and your mother so that you will live a long time in the land that the Lord your God is going to give you" (NCV). Special privileges such as a small piece of candy or a trip to a treasure box encourage good behavior.

Consistency

As children's leaders, we all have our good days and bad days. Ideally, when you arrive at church for ministry, you will be rested and ready. However, life often gets in the way: You wake up late because the neighbor's dog kept you up all night barking; on the way to church, you spill your coffee on yourself; and as you walk in the church door, you realize you left the materials for the object lesson on the kitchen counter. Not surprisingly, you're tired and frustrated. At this point, the last thing you want is to referee the Jones twins on the front row who think it is fun to punch each other in the arm to see who cries first!

On such days, we lose patience over the smallest things. At this point, we must rely on the expectations and consequences we already have in place. Conversely, when we're having a good day, we don't need to let things slip out of control.

Be consistent with whom you enforce the rules. In other words, don't pick favorites. You will readily connect with certain kids more than with others; it's only natural. Yet, you must guard against the temptation to overlook those kids' misbehavior.

Additionally, be consistent with your expectations and consequences with the lead pastor's kids, staff members' kids, and, most of all, your own kids. Just because their parents have leadership roles at the church doesn't give them a pass to do and act as they please in your ministry. Other kids will pick up on this and resentment will build, causing more problems. Also, don't expect them to be perfect either. You should hold them to the same standards as you do everyone else in your ministry.

When you establish a loving and caring discipline strategy, it provides both children and parents with a secure learning environment, and you have fewer "McDonald's Sundays."

13 Welcoming the New Kid

Steve Burkowske

So often in ministry we talk about "first impressions" that will help to draw people to our churches and keep them once they arrive. We make every effort to create a welcoming environment and friendly atmosphere to help people feel right at home.

It's the same for kids who visit our children's ministries. Whether it's a small-group setting like a Sunday school class or a large group like kids church, newcomers need a few things to be in place if they are going to come back. Before new kids will trust in you and your team, become teachable, and accept your influence in their lives, they need to feel safe, know they are liked, and be certain they are going to have fun. Without those three elements, it will be difficult to win them over.

A Safe Place

Creating a safe environment for children has to be a top priority. An effective check-in system, a security team posted throughout the facilities, and even having security cameras installed in the nursery and children's classrooms bring comfort to parents and the church's insurance agent. However, these do not concern the new child. A child feeling safe in a new environment requires intentional planning on the part of the children's pastor or teacher.

Try to imagine yourself in the newcomer's position—look through their eyes. What do you see when you approach your classrooms or ministry event?

Also, think about what a child might experience at places where children enjoy themselves (such as theme parks and child-friendly party places and restaurants). What can you learn by looking through that lens?

Keep in mind that every child is different, with particular personalities and temperaments. Also, remember the children who have physical limitations or other special needs.

When a child makes his or her first grand entrance into your children's ministry, make sure there is something that catches their eye in a positive way. Children are naturally attracted to what they see. Do they see a smile on your face? Do they see other happy kids? Do they see a clean room? Now that last one may seem odd, considering most kids are naturally messy. Aside from modeling excellence for all the children, a clean and organized space feels more comfortable for the new kids, thus feeling safer.

Also, recognize the importance of presenting an atmosphere of order and not chaos. If a child walks in on a room of girls screaming and boys roughhousing, they will probably be quick to reattach themselves to Mama's leg. I'm not suggesting to avoid a fun activity, but it must be organized and supervised. Make sure your team is in place and engaged.

A Friendly Place

Now that you have the new kid in the room, make sure the child knows he or she is liked. Children, at some point or another, will experience the insecurity of wondering if others will like them. Experience has shown that the quickest way to get new kids comfortable is to show them they are liked. The first thing I try to do is introduce the newcomer to a child close to his or her age. I typically have in my mind a list of kids whom I know will be friendly, and then I ask them to show around the new kids. Kids know what their peers are interested in, so let the more experienced kids serve as your tour guides.

Next, offer a public welcome/introduction in front of the whole group. At my church, we call this "welcoming first-time friends." Your first instinct might say not to do this, since it could be embarrassing for the child; and it can be if not done right. I am not suggesting you force a child to do anything he or she does not want to do. If a child doesn't want to participate in a welcome ceremony, that's OK. This could indicate the child may need more positive attention to get comfortable in your classroom or worship service.

I invite all the "first-time friends" to the front of kids church together. I ask them their name, age, grade, and school. When they say their name, the rest of the kids are prompted to respond with "We're glad you're here, Josh" or "Hello, Ellie." Kids like to have their peers give them a "shout out," and it keeps the rest of the kids engaged.

Next, I point out commonalities the newcomers have with other kids in the room. ("Raise your hand if you go to their school.") Giving the new kid a sense of familiarity is a definitive win.

Anytime a child says they are 7 years old, I give this resounding proclamation (and the kids say it with me): "Seven? . . . Seven? . . . *Seven* might be God's favorite number!" Admittedly it's almost obnoxious, but it always puts a smile on everyone's face. I think it's because that statement immediately shows the new child that God likes them. Anything I can do to make a new kid smile helps divert any insecurities he or she might have.

A Fun Place

If you help a child feel safe and liked, then the walls are down and it's going to be a lot easier for him or her to have fun.

Don't tune out now. I know church isn't supposed to be all fun and games. However, if your children's ministry operates *without* fun and games, you are doing yourself and the kids a great disservice. If a child doesn't have fun, you haven't won them over, and barring their parents forcing their return, that child may not be back.

Besides, you should want to have fun, and so should your team. There are so many ways to integrate fun into your class or kids church, so I won't make a list. I will, however, point out key areas to insert "fun."

First, make sure there are elements of fun in your space. Whether it's game stations, air-hockey tables, and the like, or upbeat music playing over a sound system, make sure you have things kids can enjoy as well as create opportunities for them to fellowship. And keep as much culturally relevant technology as possible in your space. If your space screams "old" or "outdated," you're going to lose.

Second, include simple but crazy games throughout the learning time. Not every game has to directly correlate with the lesson, but it helps when it does. Keep each game simple, and stop playing while everyone is still enjoying it.

If you focus on creating a safe atmosphere, helping children feel liked, and providing fun, you'll be well on your way to seeing many new kids come back.

Leading Children to Christ

Lance Colkmire

When can a child become a Christian? Some churches wait until children reach a particular age (such as 12) before trying to convert them, while others attempt to make conversions as early as the preschool years. Some churches are not convinced that a child is a believer unless he or she has had a radical conversion; others believe that such conversions are unnecessary for children who are brought up in a Christian home. Some believe that child evangelism is best accomplished through intergenerational church and family life; others evangelize children through kids crusades, children's church and other specialized means.

How should we approach child evangelism? In light of Scripture and the nature of children, how and when should we strive to win our kids to Christ?

Age of Accountability

While the Bible clearly teaches accountability, saying "each of us will give an account of himself to God" (Rom. 14:12), it does not teach that there is or is not an age of accountability. This is not a Biblical term. However, the belief that God will not condemn young children for sin they are incapable of understanding or even being aware of is consistent with the gracious and merciful God that Scripture portrays. This position can be outlined as follows:

1. Children are sinners in need of regeneration and can be saved only through Christ.

2. However, small children have a relative innocence in comparison with those who have willfully and knowingly sinned.

3. "Children are included in the great atoning sacrifice, and belong to Jesus Christ until they deliberately refuse Him" (John Inchley, *Kids and the Kingdom*).

The Nature of Salvation

In their relative state of innocence, it might seem odd to think of children as being in need of a new beginning. But just as surely as Nicodemus apparently led a moral life outside of Christ yet needed to be "born again" (John 3:3), so children who are outside of Christ are in need of redemption.

In His discussion with Nicodemus (John 3), "Jesus used two images: water and wind. The first stands for the Word of God, the second for the Holy Spirit. He is teaching that as the Word is shared, taught, preached or otherwise made known, the Holy Spirit uses it to bring forth new spiritual life in those whom God is saving" (James Montgomery Boice, *Awakening to God*).

When the Word and the Spirit move upon an individual's heart, his saving response is faith. "From God's side, it is the work of the Spirit; from [the human] side it is faith. Yet that faith itself is not any independent work; it is the work of the Holy Spirit in my heart," said Leslie Newbigin (*Sin and Salvation*).

While children by nature are quick to believe in the gospel story and the love of Christ, there still must be supernatural impartation of faith for them to savingly know Christ. Perry Downs said some people who try to win children to Christ "actually misrepresent the true nature of saving faith. . . . What does it mean to 'receive' Jesus in the sense of John 1:12? It means not simply the reception of the benefits of His substitutionary death on our behalf, but rather the reception of Him, the risen Lord" (*Christian Education Journal*).

Accepting Christ as Lord involves repentance—turning from sin and turning to God. It means not only forgiveness of sin but also forsaking the practice of sin, through the grace of God. In children's terminology, repentance means more than saying, "I'm sorry." Repentance means being sorrowful for one's sin. This is a gracious work of the Holy Spirit. "Godly sorrow brings repentance that leads to salvation" (2 Cor. 7:10).

Children cannot be saved by virtue of their physical birth into a Christian family, by an emotional response to a story or message (which is typical of children), nor by the will of their parents. As with all who accept Christ, children can only be saved "by grace . . . through faith" (Eph. 2:8).

The Biblical Perspective

There is no explicit Biblical account of a child's conversion to Christ. However, the New Testament does contain references which indicate that there were children who were believers.

In Colossians 3:20, Paul instructed children to obey their parents "in everything." Peter O'Brien observed, "The obedience of Christian children to their parents is all of a piece with their submission to Christ" (*Word Biblical Commentary, Vol. 44*).

In Ephesians 6:1, children are commanded to obey their parents "in the Lord." This apparently was a call to children to obey their parents inasmuch as their obedience would be "consistent with Christian commitment," Leslie Mitton said. "[This passage] appears to have in mind a situation where the children addressed may have had pagan parents." This would indicate that children were able to experience conversion in their own right, apart from Christian parents (*The New Century Bible Commentary*).

Writing about this same passage, William Coble said, "There is no indication of the age of those children whom Paul addressed, except the suggestion that they were still in their formative years. Whether they were to be disciplined and instructed in the Lord because they were already believers, or in order that they might become believers, is not clear" (*Childhood and Conversion*).

In Ephesians 6:4 and Colossians 3:21, parents are warned that they have the potential of turning their children away from Christ by embittering or exasperating them. But parents also have the potential of rearing their children in the "training and instruction of the Lord," thereby pointing them to Christ.

The power of parental influence is seen in the life of Timothy, who had a devout Christian grandmother and mother. The "genuine faith" by which they lived was also birthed in Timothy (2 Tim. 1:5 NKJV). Paul told Timothy, "From childhood you have known the Holy Scriptures, which are able to make you wise for salvation through faith which is in Christ Jesus" (2 Tim. 3:15 NKJV). The apostle was not saying that Biblical instruction had saved Timothy. Rather, this knowledge had equipped Timothy to be in a position where the Holy Spirit could quicken the Word to his heart, bringing him to salvation.

It is evident from these passages that children can receive Christ, and that the primary place for child evangelism and spiritual nurture is not the church, but the home.

The Question of Readiness

This brings us back to the question posed at the beginning of this chapter: When can boys and girls become Christians? Let's ask more specifically, What must children understand to be able to come to Christ? What should they feel? How must they respond?

Understanding

Children need to understand the following truths: (1) They are sinners. (2) The punishment for sin is eternal death. (3) Jesus died to take the punishment for their sin; then He arose. (4) By believing in Jesus and turning away from their sin, they receive eternal life.

Paul Meier said, "I believe some children can understand enough during the latter part of their first six years to know that they are frequently sinful, that they want God to forgive them, and that they want to live forever in heaven—and they put their simple faith in Christ" (*Christian Child Rearing and Personality Development*).

Emotions

Jesus said, "No one can come to me unless the Father who sent me draws him" (John 6:44). This "drawing" involves emotions. The child is convicted of his sinfulness while he or she is also attracted by the love of Christ. Evidence that a child is under conviction might include the following: having exaggerated fears, asking lots of questions regarding spiritual things, showing sorrow over shortcomings, and becoming either sluggish or overly active.

Genuine conviction will come as a result of the influence of the Word of God and the ministry of the Spirit of God; it will not come from mere human effort.

Faith

The proper human response for children who are beginning to understand the gospel and who are being drawn by the Holy Spirit is to believe—to put their faith in God. Eugene Chamberlain said a child can "really believe" when

- the Holy Spirit moves in his life
- his motives for receiving Christ are internal, not external
- he accepts the basic truths of the gospel
- he recognizes his accountability toward God
- his attitude toward the claims of Christ peaks in a genuine desire to live in a way to please God from this day forward ("When Can a Child Believe?").

The Challenge

Here are the four basics we've established so far:

1. Children are sinners.
2. Children belong to Christ until they willfully turn away from Him.
3. Passages from the Epistles imply that there were children in New Testament times who received Christ.
4. Children come to Christ as the Word and the Holy Spirit enlighten their understanding, draw them to Christ, and enable them to believe.

In light of those truths, our efforts at evangelizing children should be twofold: (1) preparing young children for the time when they will be enabled to receive

Christ and (2) clearly and forthrightly presenting the gospel to them when they are capable of acting upon it.

Preevangelizing Children

Since young children cannot understand the concepts of sin, salvation and personal accountability, they are not in danger of being condemned to hell. Thus, our responsibility is not to try to evangelize them but, instead, to *preevangelize* them—to teach them basic truths about God that will help to prepare their hearts for the time when the Holy Spirit will draw them to Christ. Those truths include the following:

- God can do anything.
- God created everything, including us.
- God loves us.
- God wants us to love Him.
- Jesus, God's Son, showed us how much God loves us.
- Jesus taught us how we should live.
- Jesus died, then arose.
- Jesus wants us to live with Him in heaven forever.

When children reach the ages of 5 and 6, we should introduce these additional truths: everyone has sinned, the punishment for sin is to be kept out of heaven, and Jesus died to take the punishment for our sin. As Eugene Chamberlain observed, "Long before they have any sense of personal guilt," many children develop the idea that "people do bad things but God forgives them" ("When Can a Child Believe?").

But our responsibility goes far beyond transmitting facts. We must live godly lives before our small children. William Hendricks said, "Our part in facilitating the faith of children is to provide for them the necessary picture of the faithful God and to nurture them in a context of truth and trust which will make their commitment to God easier" (*A Theology of Children*).

Evangelizing Children

Because of the way God has made children, it is relatively easy for them to put their faith in Christ. Children . . .

- generally believe what they are told
- are humble and dependent
- have tender hearts
- are teachable.

While the Holy Spirit does not draw some children to Christ until they are older, the church and home should begin to present the gospel to children during their early school years (ages 6 through 8). This must be done both informally (through example) and formally (by instruction).

Presenting the Gospel by Example

1. We teach "God loves you" by accepting and loving children unconditionally—the way God loves them.

2. We teach that all were born into sin by testifying about our alienation from God.

3. We teach that Jesus changes lives by following Christ and testifying about our conversion.

4. We teach that we have received the promise of eternal life by storing up treasure in heaven rather than on earth.

Presenting the Gospel Through Instruction

1. Explain religious terminology. Words like *sin*, *believe* and *confess* must be explained the way kids think—literally and specifically. For instance, we can define *sin* as "breaking God's commandments," but we also must list specific commandments that kids break, such as lying, hating, and cursing.

2. Don't try to "help" the Holy Spirit convict children. It is easy but wrong to manipulate kids.

3. Teach that conversion requires commitment. Don't reduce the "conceptual content of what is required in a genuine experience of conversion to a minimal 'Do you love Jesus?' kind of questioning" (William Hendricks). One way to approach the subject of commitment is by saying, "It is more than likely that you have loved Jesus for as long as you can remember. If so, I want to help you to know Him better. If not, I want to show you how to begin" (John Inchley, *Kids and the Kingdom*).

4. Teach what really happened when Christ was crucified. In so doing, we will help children understand (1) the enormity of their sin and what it cost God and (2) the endless depth of God's love. This will help children "understand both God's judgment and God's mercy" (Leslie Newbign, *Sin and Salvation*).

5. Let the children ask questions. Then help them find Biblical answers.

In the home, parents can evangelize their children by having family devotions, answering their children's questions about salvation, praying with their children, and talking with them about their experiences at church.

At church, child evangelism can take place through corporate worship services, children's church, classes, kids crusades, and VBS. In all of this, the church should work closely with the home.

Responding to a Child's Faith Profession

When a child makes a profession of faith, how do we know it is genuine? Just as is the case with an adult's testimony, we have to admit that only God knows the heart. So how should we respond to a child's profession?

First, we should neither discount nor affirm a testimony on the basis of a child's emotional response. Some children weep bitter tears of remorse when they accept Christ; some exude joy; others show little emotional response. Any of those responses can be appropriate, yet none of them proves that the child is sincere. The real question is, Has the child trusted Christ for salvation?

Second, we should not discount a testimony because the child does not have a Damascus Road experience. Some adults will not believe a child has been converted unless they see a Saul-to-Paul transformation. While true conversion will bring about change, sometimes the change is subtle. The "good" boy or girl may have an attitude change that is not easily detected from the outside. The "bad" kid may not abandon every wrong overnight, but needs to grow.

Third, we must follow up on every profession. We must talk with the child to see if he or she really understands what a commitment to Christ means. If he has confessed his sins, repented and given himself to Christ, we should affirm that God's Word teaches he is now a child of God. If the child has not yet made a commitment to Christ, we should affirm whatever positive step he has taken.

Fourth, we must nurture the converted child. When a child accepts Christ, our responsibility to his spiritual life really just begins. We must nurture his commitment, helping this child of God to "grow in the grace and knowledge of our Lord and Savior Jesus Christ" (2 Peter 3:18).

The Gospel in One Verse—A Salvation Message

You need a black marker, five sheets of poster board (a yellow one, a dark blue one, a white one, and two sheets of red) and three kids—one wearing a yellow shirt or blouse, another wearing red, and a third wearing dark blue. You also need a large white shirt or coat. Write the various portions of John 3:16 on different pieces of poster board:

- red: God so loved the world
- red: that he gave his one and only Son
- white: that whoever believes in him
- blue: shall not perish but
- yellow: have eternal life

Can anyone quote John 3:16? *Let several kids have the opportunity to try. Then have everyone say it together.*

If we look carefully at John 3:16, we will see how we can live forever with Jesus.

Display the yellow poster.

How many of you want to live forever in heaven? The Bible says Jesus is in heaven preparing a place for those who love Him. Jesus told His disciples, "In my Father's house are many rooms. . . . I am going there to prepare a place for you" (John 14:2).

Why do you think the words "have eternal life" are printed on yellow—let's call it gold—poster board? (Because heaven's streets are pure gold.) Think about how awesome heaven must be if even the paths we'll walk on are solid gold!

Have the child who is wearing yellow to come forward to represent heaven. Give him or her the yellow sign. Let's let the gold this person is wearing remind us of the place we want to live forever—heaven.

Display the "God so loved the world" poster.

What do you suppose the word *world* means in this scripture? (It means all the people in the world.) How does God feel toward all the people in the world? (He loves everyone.) That's why this part of John 3:16 is printed on red poster board—because red reminds me of love.

Have the child dressed in red to come forward. Give him the sign and have him stand next to the child wearing yellow. Not only do we want eternal life, but God himself wants us to have eternal life. He loves us and wants us to be with Him in heaven forever.

Display the blue sign. This part of the verse is printed on blue poster board because of the word *perish*. When we say someone is "blue," what do we mean? (They are very sad.) *Perish* is a very sad word. It means to die.

Have the person who is wearing dark blue come forward and stand next to you. Give him or her the blue sign. This person, just like all the rest of us, has sinned. What do we deserve because we have sinned? (We deserve death.) The Bible says the wages of sin is death. We all have broken God's laws that are written in the Bible, so we all deserve to go to hell to perish forever.

Have the person wearing blue to stand across the room from those wearing yellow and red, with the yellow being the farthest away.

Our sins keep us away from heaven and God. He still loves us, but He can allow no sinful people into heaven to ruin its perfection. But wait: this verse says "shall not perish"! God has done something so we can become new people who can indeed go to heaven.

Display the sign reading "that he gave his one and only Son."

Why do you think we chose red for these words? (First, God's giving was an act of love; second, God's Son shed His blood so our sins could be taken away.)

Give the child wearing red this poster so that he or she is now holding both red signs in the correct sequence.

God gave us His Son so our sins could be forgiven and we could have eternal life. But look—there is still a problem. Our sin can still keep us separated from God. There is something we must do if we want to live forever in heaven.

Display the white poster board.

What did Jesus promise to "whoever believes in him"? (Eternal life.) This is what happens to all who put their trust in Jesus: the blood of Jesus washes away their sin and makes them ready for heaven. They become pure—free from sin. That is why these words are written on clean, white poster board.

Give the white sign to the child holding the blue sign. Have him hold the signs in the correct sequence. Next, have this child walk across the room to stand next to the person wearing red.

This person has asked Jesus to take away his sins and make him a new person, and Jesus has done it. *Place the white shirt or coat over the child's blue shirt.*

This person has been connected with God and His love, and now he has the promise of eternal life in heaven.

Now have this child move to stand between the red and the yellow.

Have you done this? Have you asked Jesus to forgive you of your sins and make you into a new person?

Now that the John 3:16 posters are in the correct position, have everyone read the verse aloud together.

God wants to take away your sin and give you eternal life. He does not want you to perish! His love, which He showed through the gift of His Son, is reaching out to you.

But the decision is yours. Do you want to become a new person? Do you want to leave your sins behind? It's up to you.

Reaching Unchurched Kids

Elaine Shreve

I stood at the casket of 10-year-old Shawanna Bledsoe, looked at her beautiful black skin and kissed her cheek for the last time. Brokenhearted, I pondered the day Shawanna received Christ, the afternoon she was baptized in water, the weekend she performed in our children's musical, the time she won a trophy at youth camp, and the way she and her brother won their parents to the church. All this took place because we sent a church bus to a housing project every Sunday to pick up Shawanna and other children. At that moment there was no doubt in my mind of the ministry that went forth to these children and no doubt of the need or reason to reach the unchurched child.

In Mark 16:15, Jesus commands, "Go into all the world and preach the good news to all creation." This command is not limited to winning adults. Nor does this verse call us to invite children for the purpose of winning their parents so the church attendance will grow! Although such growth will be a way God blesses the church, the primary motive of reaching out to a child must be to reach and disciple that child. We must reach children where they are—show up in their world of sin and help them desire to join us in our world of redemption.

Meeting the Needs of the Unchurched Child

The ministries your church provides will vary according to its geographic location. However, the basic needs of the unchurched child do not vary. The two basic needs that cannot be neglected when ministering to the unchurched child are discipleship and love.

Discipleship: Meeting the Need for Family

If you were taken to church by your parents, the church served your family by helping to disciple you through providing role models and teaching the Word. You and your immediate family were part of the larger church family. Church is a comfortable place for children who have their families with them.

However, the unchurched child will typically feel lonely and insecure in a church setting where he or she is without family. Children who are brought in from low-income neighborhoods are often looking for ways to fulfill their desire for family. Their need for a more complete home environment is typically strong because many come from single-parent homes. This fact is painfully proven by the gang involvement seen throughout low-income housing areas. Everyone needs the security, love and commitment that a family provides.

The church has a great responsibility to these children because God has wonderful plans for their lives. Sitting among these kids are potential pastors, teachers, evangelists, and more. Of course, unchurched children need much attention and discipleship if the ministry to them is to have long-term effects. Young converts must have a spiritual parent to teach them how to apply God's Word to the world they live in.

From my personal experience growing up in a loving Catholic home, my family was functional in giving me the security, love, and commitment I needed. But when I converted from Catholicism, I felt the void of a church family in my life. I needed the witness of a godly grandmother, a spiritual sister, and a sanctified father in my new family. The church—specifically, my pastor's family—met those needs for me and then personally discipled me as a new convert.

Love: Meeting the Physical Needs

Children from non-Christian homes are sometimes "ripped" out of bed and "tossed" on a church bus. They may come to a Sunday-morning church service without breakfast. Others may come dazed and needing a hug and a few gentle words.

I taught preschoolers for several years on Wednesday evenings. During the summer they would come to church directly from playing outside all day. Three- and four-year-olds would jump on our church bus and come to class with dirty feet, faces, and hands. So I would start my class with a washcloth, restroom break, and then a snack; finally would come songs and a lesson. It sometimes took 30 minutes to clean 25 children and give them a snack, and class lasted only an hour. I struggled with the fact I was taking the time away from the Bible teaching and spending it in snack time. I decided not to serve snacks one week. And Antonio, a typically passive child, threw a tantrum! Sadly, I learned he was upset because his church snack was his only promise of dinner.

The physical needs of unchurched children need to be considered and met. Those needs will vary according to the time of day the service is held and the type of community in which you are ministering. Are you doing a street service in the middle of the summer? Consider serving a cold cola first. If it's cold outside, how about serving warm doughnuts and hot chocolate?

This is the way Jesus ministered. He never just said "I love you" without showing His love in a tangible form. Jesus fed the multitude a meal and even stopped to lay His hands on children. As we touch unreached children, we need to give them the truth of the Word and show them the unconditional love of Christ as well. Sometimes that unconditional love is revealed in the form of a snack and a cup of orange drink.

S.W.E.A.T. (Seek, Win, Expect, Assign, Teach)

Before you even begin evangelism, make sure you have some spiritual food for the children to eat. You will have problems if you bring in children and offer them a boring service to sit through. If your evangelism is on the streets as a sidewalk Sunday school, the kids won't come the second time if the first time wasn't worth it. So, don't start until you have a banquet ready.

How does a church start a child evangelism program? If there is no low-income housing project in your town, you may think there is no need to reach out to children. Maybe you think you could find only 10 children to bring, so why bother? No matter what kind of community the Lord has called you to serve, your church should be involved in evangelism. Maybe you won't be able to run three busses and fill them with screaming children, and perhaps your church doesn't even have a van, but there is something you can do to reach the children in your community.

Seek Them

"Go out to the roads . . . and make them come in" (Luke 14:23).

Kids Bringing Kids. There are two ways to start getting children to visit your church. First, ask the regular attendees to bring their friends from their neighborhoods and schools. Tell them, "If you bring a friend, you may choose a great prize from the treasure chest."

After you receive a first-time visitor's address, send that child a card. If possible, visit him or her. If that's not feasible, call the child's home. Talk with the parents. Even if the parents don't want to come to your church, you can develop a relationship with them. When children know their parents and teachers not only know each other but talk to each other too, fewer discipline problems arise.

Going to the Kids. Wherever there are houses, there are certainly some with children. When you select an area for outreach, visit door to door. Surprise people by not inviting them to church right away. Just tell them who you are and who you are with, and give them the church's phone number. Let them know that if they ever need you, they can call. Tell them about the services your church offers (food assistance, clothes closet, literacy program, Bible classes, prayer, hospital visitation, etc.).

You are ready to schedule your first outreach service when you have some unreached children who will attend. Pass out flyers announcing your upcoming service. Be sure to include your church name and address as well as your name and phone number. If you are sending vans or buses, arrange stops at central locations. If you choose a street service, locate it centrally so the children can walk. (In a street service setting, you will benefit by keeping your services high energy, entertaining, and brief.) Get as many names and addresses of the attendees as you can from your first service. Visit the home of each child you receive an address for. In fact, you should make visitation a weekly effort so that your commitment and familiarity can breed trust.

You won't meet new children just by sitting in the church. You have to go where the children are. The goal is to build relationships so you can be a Christlike model who helps to meet children's needs.

Win Them

"I have become all things to all so that . . . I might save some" (1 Cor. 9:22).

It is imperative that a child attending church for the first time be given an opportunity to accept Christ. At every altar service present the salvation message. I made the decision to always explain the plan of salvation and pray the sinner's prayer when I realized the magnitude of the message I carry as a minister to unchurched children. Honestly, you may have only one chance. The child you have brought to your church or who sits on a tarp in front of your portable stage may only hear the message of Christ one time. Children in poverty are fighting for their lives. For that reason, each week have a program of excellence that ministers to children.

What must we do to provide for the children's needs? What are their needs? Maybe you need to serve them breakfast first in order to quiet their stomach rumblings. My needs as a bus rider weren't physical, but emotional. I was won by unconditional love. That is what I was hungry for. My pastor's family loved me just the way I was. I needed Jesus, not food. When I ministered to children in the city, I found out they needed food, warm clothes in the winter, and tons of safe hugs. Most of all, they needed Jesus' love to fill a void that food or toys wouldn't touch.

When we first begin evangelism, we want to hurry up and reach lots of children. (Children's church is more fun when you have 100 kids!) But to have a valid evangelistic program we must focus on the children individually—it's people before programs. We need to win individuals to Jesus. These children are often times referred to collectively as "the bus kids" or "those kids." If we have a name, face, and an address for each child, we can begin winning the children.

Expect Them

"Look after the orphans" (James 1:27).

Did that child you visited last week come to the service today? If he did, make sure he has a good time. Evangelistic programs are often understaffed with workers but overloaded with children. Consequently, the personal touch following a big service is sometimes difficult, but it is always important. Be sure you give your time and attention to the children and deal with any worker-related issues when the children have gone home. Make sure your workers understand that they get your time before the children arrive or after the children leave.

If a child that you visited didn't come, continue to visit or call for three or four weeks in a row. If that child never comes, it's okay to move on, letting the child know that the church is still available and will send a van by his house if he calls. Keep the non-attender's address on file for mailouts regarding children's crusades and other special events.

When a new child does come, send a welcome letter and follow up with a phone call and a visit. Try to meet the parents as soon as possible. The children that become regular attendees should be permanently added to an attendance list. (At our church, they become "regulars" after three weeks of attendance.) Don't be discouraged about a high number of absentees. It's difficult for children to get up on their own. They haven't been given an example of faithful church attendance by their family.

Assign Them

"Faith by itself, if it is not accompanied by action, is dead" (James 2:17).

How would the adults in your congregation respond if all the church leadership changed every week? Imagine coming in Sunday and seeing a different pastor, different music minister, and a surprise Sunday school teacher. If that were reality, relationships would not develop . . . and we need relationships. Children need relationships, too. This goes back to the basic need for family. Children need someone who knows about them—their struggles and successes. Children need to see familiar faces and feel love from those people.

Assign the regularly attending children to adults in the congregation. This is very important to the longevity of the child's relationship with the Lord and with the church. Each of these adults will be a mentor who loves "their" child, identifies with him, and calls him by name. The children's pastor must not be the only person who knows the children. How can one person effectively disciple dozens of children? Jesus was perfect, yet He had only 12 disciples!

The children's pastor should solicit help from other leaders in the church. The leaders can discover the needs of the children and report them to the children's pastor. Outreach workers need the love and support of the children's pastor. Worker training will ultimately help retain the children. The children's pastor should regularly communicate with the workers through e-mails, text messages, and meetings.

Dealing with unchurched children can be difficult. Often there are behavior problems that can discourage workers. I have found that a worker who visits the children's homes with me is a worker that will stay with me. Pick a visitation day—such as a particular Saturday from 10:00 a.m. until 12:00 noon. Give visitation assignments. Be deliberate and time conscious. Once a worker has visited a child's home environment, they will have a greater understanding of the child. They will feel the responsibility of ministering to the children on a more personal level.

Teach Them

"Hold to the teachings we passed on to you" (2 Thess. 2:15).

I remember seeing my parents take an envelope to Mass every Sunday. This was instilled in me by example, but I had to ask my Pentecostal teachers why. The children whose parents have never set foot in the church have no idea about supporting a church with their finances. This is one of many areas in which the need for personal discipleship is necessary.

Without a Christian heritage, your children will not know how to honor their pastor or how to behave in the sanctuary. We want them to become church members and raise their families in a church. That doesn't mean we have to dress each kid in a suit or a dress and put a giant cross around their neck. The goal is to teach the Word of God with the intent of changing lives. This takes much time and personal attention.

Endure

"We continually remember before our God and Father your work produced by faith, your labor prompted by love, and your endurance inspired by hope in our Lord Jesus Christ" (1 Thess. 1:3).

Perhaps the most difficult part of evangelism is the frustration of the unseen. Because we can't see into the spiritual realm, we do not always feel effective. Growing a children's evangelism ministry will take time. If you are frustrated with the process, it will show. Write down milestones when they are achieved—document your progress so that year after year you can be reminded of God's faithfulness. Many times the funds are low, there is a worker shortage, and there are unpredictable attendance drops. These all feel like three strikes against you. And we haven't even mentioned the spiritual warfare! As you document, you will see the progress. If you quit because you miss your Sunday school class or because no one is helping you, you aren't enduring.

An enduring ministry will disciple broken children into healed, educated, and loved children of God. If you have 100 children today and an empty church in 12 years, what have you done? Effective outreach will be slow and steady because we are prioritizing people before programs.

"Let us not grow weary while doing good, for in due season we shall reap if we do not lose heart" (Gal. 6:9 NKJV).

WHEN UNCHURCHED CHILDREN COME TO CHURCH

Dan Jenkins

The following words often echo through my mind as if I heard them with my own ears: "Let the little children come to Me, and do not forbid them; for of such is the kingdom of heaven" (Matt. 19:14 NKJV).

Jesus Christ was telling His disciples not to shoo the children away but instead to lead them to Him. This parallels the calling God places on children's pastors—to partner with parents in leading children to Jesus.

Here are some questions we must ask: What about those children whose parents are not part of the process? What about those who are dropped off, picked up on a bus, or find another way to the house of God? Is it not our calling to lead them to Jesus?

Ministering to the unchurched child has its own set of difficulties and challenges. According to the Billy Graham Evangelistic Association, "A change has taken place over the last 30 years in this country. There are more kids who, if they're not 'churched,' are likely to be woefully ignorant of Jesus and the gospel. It used to be that there was at least one family member who went to church. Now we're in a generation where often nobody in a family has ever been inside of a church."

It is our job to identify these challenges and work to resolve them. Here are three of the resolutions I've made over ten years of full-time children's ministry: I will (1) build relationships, (2) communicate clearly, and (3) discipline lovingly.

Build Relationships

Building relationships is a top priority in ministry—even more so in reaching the unchurched. Taking time to learn a person's story gives us insight into how we can best minister to him or her. Telling our story allows others to see we are human, sharing some of the same fears, passions, and temptations they face. This also opens opportunities to tell God's story.

Another way to build relationships is to get involved in children's lives outside of church. Let them see you attending their school programs, sporting events, recitals, and so on. This has given me opportunities to meet unchurched family members, showing them I really do care about them and their children.

Communicate Clearly

Communication is a key in any relationship. Unchurched children are not going to understand "Christian-ese" (the language of the church). The Lord impressed on my heart several years ago to make each moment in my service a teaching moment—explaining Bible truths in kid-friendly ways.

Unchurched kids need to know *what* we are doing but, most importantly, *why* we are doing it. At first, they will not always know how to communicate properly in return. That will take time to develop.

Another key factor in communication is collaboration. All team members must work together to effectively reach unchurched kids. Setting clear policies, procedures, and strategies, as well as clearly communicating the vision with those who work both directly and indirectly with you, will elevate the level of effectiveness.

Discipline Lovingly

Unchurched children will not know how they are supposed to act at church—what is acceptable and what is not. With behavioral issues, take a hint from Deputy Barney Fife—make sure you "nip it in the bud." If you're not careful, you will spend more time correcting and less time communicating the gospel.

Clear and consistent guidelines are necessary. Most of these children probably come from homes where discipline is inconsistent. They are coming to a place that is most likely very different from where they just came from. Think about this: You will often teach something contrary to what these children are seeing and hearing at home.

These children need to experience more than the negative side of you in discipline; they need to see that you genuinely care. Don't only use negative discipline strategies, but balance them with a positive reward system. Do not embarrass children publicly, but always publicly acknowledge their positive behavior.

Expelling a kid from church should always be a last resort. After all, church is where they need to be. Patience is a must, but it cannot be at the expense of the other students' safety or learning experience.

Keep Shining

Through building relationships, establishing consistency, and focusing on positive rewards and recognition, you will begin to see some unchurched students grow in their relationship with God. Continually offering opportunities to bring the whole family into your facility will also aid in this process. One way I do this is by offering grand-prize drawings after large events where individuals must be present the following service to be eligible.

Every effort we make helps us shine the light of Jesus. God has called some to plant and others to water, but God gives the increase (1 Cor. 3:6-7).

Helping Kids Develop a Devotional Life

Lance Colkmire

Helping children develop a private devotional life "is one of the most neglected areas in Christian education of children," says Eleanor Hance.

She continues, "One reason may be that children need continual and close adult guidance and supervision to begin and sustain a practice which they must carry on as individuals. They are rarely sufficiently self-motivated or skilled or persevering by themselves. . . . From inadequate guidance springs unfruitful practice which can soon lead to discouragement. It takes much effort and know-how to teach private worship" (*Childhood Education in the Church*).

She's right. Equipping children to pray and read God's Word on their own isn't easy. Consequently we tend to deal with the issue in a shallow way—merely exhorting children to pray and read the Word, without actually helping them put it into practice.

However, it is our duty as ministers to children to help them put on the whole armor of God, which includes the sword of the Spirit and the weapon of prayer (Eph. 6:17-18).

Here are five reasons why it is critical that we do all we can to help children practice private devotions:

1. Children need to know how much God loves them.
2. Children need to learn to hear God's voice.
3. Children need to cast their cares on the Lord.

4. Children need to be equipped to fight the Enemy.
5. God wants to move through the prayer lives of children.

Teaching Children to Pray

Providing a Model

When the disciples asked Jesus, "Lord, teach us to pray," He responded by giving them a model prayer to follow. As recorded in Matthew 6:9-13 (KJV), this prayer contains the following elements:

- Worship: "Our Father which art in heaven, hallowed be thy name. . . . For thine is the kingdom, and the power, and the glory, for ever."
- Confession: "Forgive us our debts, as we forgive our debtors."
- Requests: "Give us this day our daily bread."
- Submission: "Thy kingdom come. Thy will be done in earth, as it is in heaven."

In teaching children how to pray, we should follow Jesus' example by providing children with a model. When I teach on prayer, I make an acrostic of the word pray, which uses action words to highlight the four elements of the Lord's Prayer:

Praise

Repent

Ask

Yield

By teaching each of these elements one at a time in a series of lessons, you take a first step in helping children to discover personal prayer. Here are outlines for teaching such a series.

PRAISE

Getting Together. Have the kids come up with praise statements which they would like to hear directed at themselves. Then let kids take turns bragging on each other. Next, mention how much God wants to hear us praise Him.

Learning the Word. Read and act out the story of the 10 lepers in Luke 17:11-19, lifting up the example of the one leper who took time to praise Jesus.

Applying the Word. Read Psalm 117 and have students name the two reasons this psalm says we should praise God. (Because He loves us so much and because He is faithful to us) Talk about specific ways in which God expresses His love and faithfulness to us.

Doing the Word. Have everyone pray aloud together, "Lord, I know You love me because _____," and take turns completing the praise statement out loud. Finally, have everyone privately give praise to God for His greatness.

REPENT

Getting Together. Make a poster-board arrow on which kids write prayer requests they have made to God during the past week. Hold the arrow facing up, letting it represent our prayers to God. Then read Psalm 66:18, which says unconfessed sin can keep our prayers on the ground. Drop the arrow to the floor.

Learning the Word. Read and act out the story of the Pharisee and the Tax Collector in Luke 18:9-14. Point out how unconfessed sin blocked the Pharisee's prayer.

Applying the Word. Read Matthew 6:5-6, which teaches us not to pray hypocritically, as the Pharisee prayed—just to show off. Instead, those who sincerely pray will do most of their praying in private. And genuine prayer always includes any necessary repentance.

Doing the Word. Remind the children of the prayer requests they wrote on the arrow. Then ask them if any sin is present that would block their prayers from getting through. Have them spread apart so they can pray privately—beginning with repentance.

ASK

Getting Together. Have children take turns acting out how they would ask various people for a favor. For example: asking a schoolteacher for an extra day to turn in a project, asking for a sports hero's autograph, asking Mom or Dad for $50, and asking a 911 operator to send an ambulance to one's home. Then ask how we should approach God with prayer requests.

Learning the Word. Read Hebrews 11:6 to identify how we should approach God with our requests. (We must come in faith, knowing that He will reward us with an answer.) Explore how God answered the prayers of three Old Testament people: Elijah (1 Kings 19:1-8); Hannah (1 Sam. 1:10, 11, 20); and Solomon (1 Sam. 3:9-13). Identify (1) what each person requested and (2) how God answered (No—I have a better plan; Yes, but wait; Yes, here and now). Point out that God's answer is always best, whether yes, no, or wait.

Applying the Word. Write the words of Philippians 4:6 on the board, circling the word petition. Point out that to *petition God* means "to come to Him as a servant would approach a mighty king"—we bring Him our requests, trusting Him to answer wisely.

Doing the Word. Divide into prayer trios and have children pray for one another's requests.

YIELD

Getting Together. Perform a skit in which one person talks continually, frustrating the other person's attempts to respond. Compare this with how some people pray—always talking but never listening for God's answer.

Learning the Word. Explain that a vital part of prayer is taking time to hear God's voice, then yielding—or saying yes—to what He says. Read the story of God's calling of young Samuel in 1 Samuel 3:1-11. Then have three volunteers take on the roles of Eli, Samuel, and the voice of God to act out the story.

Applying the Word. On the board, write Samuel's response when he realized God was speaking to him: "Speak, Lord, for Your servant is listening." Pass out pieces of construction paper which you have cut into the shape of an ear. Have the kids write Samuel's response on it. If they are ready to follow Samuel's example by taking time to listen to God and then to yield, have them sign their name below Samuel's words.

Doing the Word. Review the four parts of prayer—*praise*, *repent*, *ask* and *yield*. Then lead the students in following this model one step at a time. Give them one minute to praise . . . one minute to repent of any wrong attitudes or actions . . . one minute to bring requests before God . . . and one minute to yield themselves unto the Lord and listen to His voice. You might choose to softly play worship music during this time.

Sending the Model Home

For the P-R-A-Y model to be one that children will use, you must review this process again and again at church, and you must practice it there with them.

As a memory jogger, make Bible bookmarks (laminating them, if possible) on which you print the four steps.

Teaching Children to Use God's Word

As with prayer, church should be a training ground where children learn how to use their "training manual"—the Bible.

First, children need to own a Bible which they can understand. Two translations that are particularly well-suited for children are the *New Century Version* and the *New Living Translation*.

Second, children need to bring their Bibles to church and use them. It's not enough for kids to merely earn points or get a sticker for bringing a Bible—they need to get their nose in it.

Robert Klausmeier suggests the following ways to have children use their Bibles in the church classroom:

- Let students find all Bible references.
- Show students the location of familiar stories.
- Stop your Bible-story presentation at crucial points and send the students into their Bibles to discover and report on the outcome.

- Read the verses before and after a memory verse or a Bible story to place it in context ("Make the Bible a Children's Book, Too," *Evangelizing Today's Child*).

Other ways to help children become familiar with God's Word are:

- Sometimes conduct a "sword drill"—how quickly can kids find a verse?
- Have older children take turns presenting a brief devotion.
- Help children learn how to use the Bible concordance and Bible dictionary in the back of the Bible.
- Teach children the books of the Bible.
- Help children to find and to pray the promises of Scripture, applying those promises to their own lives.

"Relate Biblical terms to modern equivalents," says Terry Hall. "For example, employees instead of servants, presidents rather than kings, or a worker's earnings for one day instead of drachmas. Which is more meaningful to today's child: to say Noah's ark measured 300 cubits, or that is was one and a half football fields long?" ("The Bible and Our World Today," *Evangelizing Today's Child*).

Be an example. Perhaps the most important thing you can do to motivate children to get into God's Word is to provide the right example by (1) conveying your own genuine excitement about Scripture, (2) living the biblical principles you teach, and (3) testifying about the power of God's Word in your life. Become the type of leader described in Hebrews 13:7: "Remember your leaders, who spoke the word of God to you. Consider the outcome of their way of life and imitate their faith."

Equipping Children to Talk with God at Home

Here are ways to encourage children to pray and read the Bible at home.

Provide devotional materials. There are many excellent devotional books available for children and their families.

Provide prayer partners. Mary Blye Howe suggests, "Assign the children to pray for someone in the class throughout the week. Ask them to exchange phone numbers and to call each other once during the week to set aside the same time to pray for each other. In class they could write down a prayer request or two on a slip of paper and give it to their prayer partner for the week" ("Young Ministers," *Evangelizing Today's Child*).

Give them an accountability tool. Give each child a stamped postcard with the numbers 1 through 10 written on one side. Each day the child has private devotions, he circles one of the numbers. When all are circled, the child signs his name and sends it back to you. Then you can provide the child with another card.

Equip them to pray God's Word. Elsie Lippy says to give the children "a list of top 10 verses for each child to keep in his Bible as a reference for specific needs such as fear (Ps. 27:1), anger (Eph. 4:32), discouragement (Josh. 1:9), decision-making (Prov. 3:5-6), assurance of salvation (1 John 5:11-12), sadness (Rom. 15:13), disappointment (Rom. 8:28), temptation (Eph. 6:10), forgiveness (1 John 1:9), loneliness (Rom. 8:38-39)." Encourage the children to read and pray the appropriate scripture in time of need ("Bible Study," Evangelizing Today's Child).

Pray for your children. Pray for the devotional lives of the children to whom you minister. Pray that they will become like the young people described in 1 John 2:14: "You are strong, and the word of God lives in you, and you have overcome the evil one."

Reaching Out to Grieving Children

Chris Knipp

A Normal Wednesday Night

It was a normal Wednesday afternoon. As a children's pastor, I was doing the usual things like . . .

- making sure the Bluebelles had enough glue for their craft project
- ensuring the Little Sweethearts had a variety of glitter for their project
- praying that the Royal Rangers were not going to make too bad of a mess doing the things boys do (sanding Pinewood Derby cars, hot-gluing miniature wooden buildings, or playing classroom kickball).
- Having communicated effectively with my teachers and meeting all of their supply requests, all was well. I was planning on having an effective and efficient Wednesday night engaging our wonderful children with the good news in creative and exciting ways. I was not planning on dealing with the news we received a couple hours before church.

The Crisis

There was a mother and her children who came to church early on Wednesday nights for piano practice. While I was prepping classrooms this particular Wednesday, the kids were in piano practice . . . and their mom was receiving the most horrible news of her life. Her husband and loving father of her kids had died in an automobile accident coming home from work.

While this woman was finding out the news downstairs, I was finding out the news upstairs from one of our other church moms walking down the hallway in tears. We hear of events like this all the time on the news, and quickly whisper prayers to God for those involved, but this was different. This was personal—it hit home. This wasn't just bad news; it was *our* tragedy.

Processing the Crisis

I knew this dad and his family. I remembered when the entire family served with our boys and girls clubs raking leaves at an elderly couple's house. "Pastor Chris, this is what being the church is all about," the dad told me with both hands leaning on his rake. This was a good man leaving behind a great family—his wife, two daughters, and a teenage son.

A flood of emotions swelled up in me in those moments. I felt an incredible gut-wrenching sadness for this family . . . a personal pain at the loss of a friend . . . an overwhelming burden to somehow comfort a family in crisis.

Taking a break from ensuring everything was ready for church that night, I found a private place to pray. I needed communion with the Spirit of God to be a vessel of His presence to the present need of a hurting family.

Being the Church

I am still not fully aware of all the information the kids knew before church time about the tragic accident. I knew they knew *something* was wrong. Mom decided to allow them to attend church with their friends before bringing them downstairs to the pastor's office to talk with them further about it.

While Mom was downstairs grieving with friends and family in the pastor's office, our Wednesday-night teachers and I were with the girls upstairs for their clubs. It was painful knowing what had happened to their father and realizing it would soon be a hard-hitting reality to these precious children. Yet, I discovered the best thing I could do to reach out and provide some comfort to these children was simply *be with them.*

At this time of crisis, this family will remember the pain, the emotions, the sadness; but they will also remember they were not alone. As children's leaders, we sometimes feel like we have to have the right words to say to minister to people who are hurting, yet one of the most important things we can do is be there. Be present in the moment of their pain. Be a shoulder to cry on and cry along with them, helping them realize they are not alone and they don't have to carry the pain alone. Be full of the Holy Spirit, letting the presence of God flow through you as it ministers to them.

Continue Being the Church

After church, we took the girls downstairs to be with their mom, their brother, and family friends. It's common at the initial stage of trauma for a child to be in shock. It can take time for the reality of events to sink in.

Children have a hard time grasping a terrible reality like death. When tragedy happens, you may not see an emotional response right away. Whether they seem emotional or not, realize it's important to be with them and to remind them God is with them and loves them.

Also, keep in mind that at the time of the crisis, their lives likely will be filled with family, friends, flowers, and a lot of attention. Yet, all these people will soon settle back into the normal patterns of their lives. So, it's important to identify ways of being involved in their lives and planning for a long process of grieving with the children and family. After the loss, it will be difficult for the family to navigate through holidays, birthdays, and anniversaries. Each special occasion will be another reminder that their loved one is no longer present, and the finality of their absence will continue to settle in deeper. As the body of Christ, we must continue to reach out with love and care while helping the family adjust to their "new normal."

Partnering in the Process

As ministers, whether vocational or volunteer, we have been called to care for the family and the children. While we offer spiritual hope, the ministry of presence and encouraging words from Scripture, we have to understand our limitations. Often, children and families that have experienced trauma will need professional counseling to continue the process of healing and recovery. We must be able to identify good Christian counselors. We must partner with them to see that these children experience spiritual, mental, and emotional healing.

Be Prepared

This real-life story was a ministry experience unlike any other I have encountered to this day. We hope such an experience will never happen, but it is wise to think through a response plan just in case. I hope the reality of my story will help you be prepared when crisis hits your ministry personally, for crisis usually hits us on *a "normal" Wednesday afternoon.*

Of course, it's not going to necessarily be on a Wednesday. However, a crisis is not worried about your routine or planning calendar. It is wise to have a crisis-management team in place to help families. It's too late to begin thinking about how to deal with the unexpected when you're in the thick of it. Be prepared. Have your team identify potential situations so you can be prepared to deal with *the crisis.*

Crises come in different shapes and sizes, but we should always respond with love and care. We need to be there. We need the Holy Spirit to work through us doing only what He can do. The Holy Spirit can help the children and family in *processing the crisis.*

In my story, I told how I found a place of prayer and began to process the crisis. When a crisis hits in your ministry, you need to have a plan and process the crisis prayerfully. When you as a leader are prepared, you will be able to help the family/child take the best first steps through the grieving process and start working their way toward wholeness.

When the crisis first hits, it is not your role to provide answers. A child just learning of the death of his or her father does not need you telling him or her this is part of God's plan. Instead, the child just needs you to be there with the presence of the Holy Spirit within you. Bearing the burden with them is *being the church.*

We're called to "bear one another's burdens" (Gal. 6:2 NKJV). We are the body of Christ; we are the Church. The Bible says, "If one member suffers, all the members suffer" (1 Cor. 12:26 NKJV). We are called to "rejoice with those who rejoice; mourn with those who mourn" (Rom. 12:15).

When you are with a child and their family in a time of crisis, you are bonding with them in an intimate way that can potentially deepen their faith through the grieving process. This is important the moment the crisis hits, but as time goes by, don't forget to *continue being the church.*

Keep loving the family and the children well beyond the initial crisis. When a little time passes, it's easy for you and others not directly affected to forget about it and move on. Remember that the hurting family will have to relive the crisis during significant moments in life. Make sure your crisis team has a plan in place to continue being the church by supporting the children throughout the extended grieving process. They'll need it.

Also, remember that you'll need *partners in the process.* We must provide spiritual nurture and support through prayer and God's Word; yet, it could prove very helpful for the child/family to receive help from a licensed Christian counselor.

A good book I recommend is *Comforting Children in Crisis* (Group Publishing). It contains a lot of practical advice to help you bring your "A game" to a crisis situation. This book offers real-life narratives, care and counseling tips, and advice on what to say and what not to say.

May God bless you as you prepare yourself to minister to hurting kids. There is a lot of pain in this world. Children and families need us to prepare ourselves to minister to them in their time of need.

Baptism, Communion, and Footwashing

Lance Colkmire

We must intentionally provide children the opportunity to take part in the ordinances of the church. We must teach kids about these vital practices and give them the opportunity to participate.

What Are the Ordinances?

"The ordinances of the church are visible signs of the saving work of Jesus Christ. They are outward representations of the great realities of salvation and confirm the divine promise of redeeming grace to believers. For believers the ordinances are not mere ceremony in worship but a means of real communion with God and of strengthening grace.

"For acts of worship to be identified as ordinances, they must be (1) instituted by Jesus himself, (2) tied to His atoning death, and (3) repeated in the church.

"The ordinances are not absolutely essential to salvation. They do not create faith, but they presuppose faith and are a response to faith (Acts 2:41; 1 Cor. 11:23-32). Ordinances are important because they are commanded by Christ and strengthen faith" (French L. Arrington, *Christian Doctrine, Volume 3*).

We believe that water baptism, the Lord's Supper, and footwashing are the ordinances Christ established and which we must preserve and observe. Failing to enable children to meaningfully take part in these ordinances means failing to challenge them to genuine discipleship.

Three Guidelines

To effectively teach children about the ordinances, we should tackle one at a time. When we teach about each one, here are three general guidelines to follow:

1. Tell the story of how Jesus established the ordinance.

2. Emphasize how participating in it is a special way to follow Jesus' example.

3. Give children the opportunity to ask questions.

Water Baptism

An important distinction between water baptism and the other two sacraments is that baptism is intended to be a one-time act in a person's life, while Communion and footwashing are to be observed regularly.

Jesus' baptism took place at the outset of his public ministry. He came to John to be baptized at the Jordan River, but John protested, saying, "I ought to be baptized by you. Why have you come to me?" Jesus responded, "For now this is how it should be, because we must do all that God wants us to do" (Matt. 3:14-15 CEV).

When Jesus was baptized, the Father himself announced that this indeed was the Son of God, shouting it from heaven! And the Holy Spirit confirmed it, coming to rest on Jesus in the form of a dove.

So, the baptism of Jesus served to declare His identity. Today, Christian baptism is a once-for-all public testimony that we now identify ourselves with Christ.

Because a Christian is to be baptized only once, it is extremely important that children understand the significance of baptism before they are baptized. We must teach them the meaning of baptism, who can be baptized, and how we are baptized.

The Meaning of Baptism

1. *We remember.* Teach children that baptism is a picture of how Jesus gave up His life for us.

   As we go down into the water, we remember Jesus' death. As we go under the water, we show how Jesus was buried in a tomb. As we come out of the water, we show how He was resurrected.

2. *We testify.* Teach children that baptism is a picture of what Jesus has done in our lives.

   As we go down into the water, we are saying Jesus died for our sins. As we go under the water, we are saying Jesus has buried our sins, never to remember them against us. As we come out of the water, we are saying that Jesus is giving us the power to live a new, resurrected life.

How We Are Baptized?

1. *In public.* Ask the boys and girls, "Why are we baptized in public instead of in secret?" (We are baptized in front of the church to show the congregation that we have asked Jesus to become our Savior and our Master.)

2. *By immersion.* Do an object lesson to demonstrate the meaning of baptize. You need a clear bowl, red dye, and a piece of white cloth cut into the shape of a person.

   Fill the bowl with the dye. Explain that the red dye reminds us that Jesus died for our sins, shedding His blood for us.

   Next, display the cloth "person." Explain that this person is pure because he has asked Jesus to take away his sins and come into his life. Now he wants to be baptized to obey Christ's command and to show everyone he has put his faith in Christ.

   Place the cloth in the dye, saying that just as the cloth will now become permanently identified with the dye, so we become identified with Jesus when we are baptized.

   We are "immersed" in baptism—we go under the water—to remind us of Jesus' death and resurrection and to show how He has changed us.

3. *In the name of the Trinity.* Have the kids read how Jesus said His disciples were to baptize people—"in the name of the Father and of the Son and of the Holy Spirit" (Matt. 28:19).

   God the Father loved us so much that He sent His Son, Jesus, to save us from our sins. Jesus loved us so much that He gave His life for us. And Jesus has sent the Holy Spirit to live with all of us who love Him. So we are baptized in the name of the Father, the Son, and the Holy Spirit.

How Do We Prepare Children for Water Baptism?

1. *Win them to Christ.* The Bible sets no minimal age limit for water baptism. The Biblical pattern is that once someone learns about Christ and receives Him as Savior, baptism follows. Once a child receives Christ, he or she is a candidate for baptism.

2. *Teach them the meaning and purpose of water baptism.* Far too many children get baptized without understanding the significance of what they are doing. This can happen at camp, in a revival, and even during a regular church service. And it's a mistake.

   While any saved child can be baptized, no child should be baptized until he or she is capable of understanding its meaning and has been taught its purpose. Remember—baptism is a one-time act that is weighted with deep meaning and spiritual blessing.

3. *Work with them individually.* Once a child has received Christ and learned the meaning of baptism, find out if the child has an interest in being

baptized at this time. If there is interest, contact the child's parents or guardian. If the parents are believers, they should be encouraged to talk with their child about baptism.

4. *Meet with the family.* Once you are in agreement with parents that their child is ready for baptism, hold a brief meeting with the family. In this meeting, have the child give his or her testimony. Review the purpose and the method of baptism. Answer any questions the children may have. The senior pastor should participate in this meeting.

5. *Plan and conduct a baptismal service.* Work with the pastor in setting the time for a baptismal service. During the service, it can be especially meaningful for the child to (1) answer a question about the meaning and purpose of baptism and/or (2) tell why he or she is getting baptized.

Four Reasons Why Some Children Do Not Get Baptized

1. *Fear.* "Will the pastor drop me?" and "Where will I change clothes?" are among the fears that some children have concerning baptism. By walking children through the baptism process, such fears can be alleviated.

2. *Embarrassment.* Some children shy away from water baptism because of embarrassment—they think they'll look ridiculous with their clothes wet or that they'll make a mistake when being baptized. Teaching them the importance of taking a stand for Jesus as well as walking them through the baptismal process can help them overcome embarrassment.

3. *No opportunity.* If there is no baptismal service on the calendar, how can someone be baptized? That is where you come in. When you as a children's pastor or leader know a child is ready for baptism, you must talk with the senior pastor about scheduling a baptismal service.

4. *Lack of understanding.* A fourth reason why some born-again kids are not baptized is that they simply have not been prepared for it.

Wrong Reasons Why Some Kids Do Get Baptized

1. *To follow the crowd.* "By best friend is getting baptized, so why shouldn't I?"

2. *Because it looks like fun.*

3. *Because of Mom or Dad's insistence.* Sometimes it's the parents we must teach! Encourage them not to push their children to be baptized unless they know their kids are spiritually and mentally prepared.

4. *Because they know it's a good thing to do.* Let's first help them discover why it's a good thing to do and whether or not they are spiritually prepared.

The Lord's Supper

Picture this: It's Sunday night at church, and a children's choir is seated in the choir loft, soon to sing. The pastor steps forward and has the elements of Communion distributed to the congregation and to people seated on the platform, but the children are not served. As the worshipers are led in receiving Communion, some of the children pick up imaginary cups and imaginary pieces of bread and do their best to join in!

This really happened! But why were the children not served? Because the pastor was concerned that they might spill grape juice as it was passed down the rows!

Sadly, this is the attitude displayed in too many churches—that children cannot meaningfully take part in the Lord's Supper! (Can you imagine an adult choir intentionally being left out?)

What should we do to see that children are able to take part in this sacred act?

Understand Who Can Receive Communion

Jesus Christ instituted Communion as a solemn observance for His children. It is a time for those who know Him to remember Him.

The Word of God exhorts Christians, "A man ought to examine himself before he eats of the bread and drinks of the cup" (1 Cor. 11:28).

Elementary-age children can so examine themselves. They can ask themselves, *Have I allowed Jesus to take away my sins?* Then they should ask, *Am I ready to seriously take part in this Communion service?*

The problem the Corinthians were having was failing to recognize "the body of the Lord" (v. 29); thus they were partaking "in an unworthy manner" (v. 27).

If a child is in relationship with Christ and is ready to thoughtfully eat the Lord's Supper, he or she can participate.

But what about small children who may not yet understand their need of salvation? Can they take part?

Young children should not be denied the privilege of partaking in Communion, nor should an unwilling child be pushed to participate. Parents should be made aware of the church's plans to have a Communion service so they may discuss it with their children in advance. If the child wants to show his or her love for Jesus by participating, parents should stress the seriousness of this event. It is not time to play; instead, it is time to quietly think about how much Jesus loves us. On the basis of his or her membership in a Christian family, the young child should be allowed to participate in this sacred act.

Teach the Meaning of Communion

1. *A symbolic act.* We must begin by teaching children that Communion is not snack time—it is not just drinking juice and eating crackers. Instead, the bread and the juice are reminders.

Jesus said when we drink the juice, we are to think of His blood. We are to remember how His blood was shed for our sins. When we eat the bread, we are to think of His body, which was beaten and crucified for our sins.

2. *A spiritual act.* Teach children that it pleases God when they take part in Communion. Here's why:

    - They're obeying Him, for Jesus told us to eat the Lord's Supper.
    - They're worshiping Him as they think about the meaning of what they are doing.
    - They're showing love to Him and thinking of how much He loves them.
    - They're becoming closer to God.

Looking Three Ways

An effective way to more fully teach children about Communion is to use a picture of a traffic light.

This traffic light will help us learn more about the Lord's Supper. Turn to 1 Corinthians 11:23-28 in your Bible. Try not to lose your place, for we will be looking at these verses at different times during the message.

1. *Remember the Cross.* Ask everyone to read the last part of verse 24 aloud: "Do this in remembrance of me."

    Next to the red light, write "STOP—Remember the Cross."

    The Lord Jesus wants us to stop and remember His death. We do this through the Lord's Supper.

    As we drink from the cup, we think of how Jesus prayed after He ate the Lord's Supper with His disciples. Jesus knew the terrible pain He would face by carrying our sins and being crucified; and as He poured out His heart to His Father, His sweat became like drops of blood.

    As Jesus prayed, He was arrested. Soon His back was being beaten by the cruel Roman whip. This whip sank deep into Jesus' back, bringing forth rivers of flesh and blood. The soldiers also rammed a crown of thorns into Jesus' skull, causing blood to pour from His head.

    As Jesus was nailed to the cross, blood came from His hands and feet. Finally, a sword was thrust into His side.

    As we eat the bread, we think of Jesus' body. We stop and remember how tired His body became as He tried to carry the cross . . . how every move He made tortured Him while His body was on the cross . . . how He hung on the cross for hours . . . and how His body slumped over in death.

    Besides stopping to remember the Crucifixion, we also remember the Resurrection. Jesus rose again with a new, perfect, everlasting body—the type of body every Christian will have in heaven.

2. *Examine yourself.* The middle light on a traffic signal is called the caution light. What is its purpose? (To warn drivers to slow down and prepare to stop.)

   Next to the middle light, write "CAUTION—Examine yourself."

   The Bible flashes a warning light—a caution—to us about taking Communion. It's found in 1 Corinthians 11:28. What is the warning? (We must examine ourselves before eating the Lord's Supper.)

   When we examine ourselves, what are we looking for? (Sin.) If we find sin in our lives, what must we do about it before we can eat the bread and drink the juice? (Confess our sin and receive God's forgiveness.)

   We become worthy to take part only when we let Jesus' blood cleanse us from our sin. Then, as we eat and drink, we can praise Jesus for shedding His blood and allowing His body to be beaten, for we have allowed His suffering to pay for our sins.

   The Bible says it is a sin for a person who won't repent to take part in the Lord's Supper. That is why there is a time of prayer for self-examination before Communion is served. At that time we can ask God's forgiveness, becoming ready to eat the bread and drink the cup.

3. *Look to the future.* The third light on the traffic signal means "Go!"

   It can remind us of two things. First, once we have examined ourselves and remembered Christ's death, we have a green light: we can go ahead and take part in Communion.

   There is something else, however. Have someone read verse 26: "For as often as you eat this bread and drink this cup, you proclaim the Lord's death till He comes" (NKJV).

   Next to the green light, write "GO—Look to the future."

   Repeat the last three words of that verse with me three times: "Till He comes."

   When we take part in Communion, we should not only look back to the time Christ suffered and died; but we should also look ahead to the day He will come again and we will go with Him to heaven.

   Christians are to practice the Lord's Supper until Jesus comes down from heaven and we go with Him to our eternal home.

Celebrating the Lord's Supper

Celebrating in Corporate Worship. It is important that there be times when children sit with their families in the sanctuary and take part in the Lord's Supper with the entire church. But there are churches where this never happens!

In a church where Communion is observed on occasional Sunday mornings alone, and where the children are always in children's church, children can never take part. This should not be!

We should intentionally plan times when children can take part in corporate Communion. This can happen . . .

- in an all-ages-together-service on Sunday morning
- with parents and kids together in a classroom
- during special midweek services (such as New Year's and Thanksgiving) when everyone comes together.

Celebrating in Kids Church. It is good to occasionally celebrate Communion in children's worship. We should teach on the meaning of Communion, and then move into the time of remembrance. Here's a suggested format for the celebration time:

1. Sing a worship chorus that focuses on Christ's sacrifice.

2. While music plays, have the children bow their heads in meditation. Allow them about a minute for self-examination. Then pray, "Dear Lord, we have examined ourselves. Please forgive us as we confess our sins. We are not worthy to take part in the Lord's Supper, but we're so happy that You make us worthy."

3. Ask how many children desire to take part in the Lord's Supper. Pass out the juice and the bread, instructing the children to simply hold them for now.

4. Have someone read 1 Corinthians 11:23-26:

   The Lord Jesus, on the night he was betrayed, took bread, and when he had given thanks, he broke it and said, "This is my body, which is for you; do this in remembrance of me." In the same way, after supper he took the cup, saying, "This cup is the new covenant in my blood; do this, whenever you drink it, in remembrance of me." For whenever you eat this bread and drink this cup, you proclaim the Lord's death until he comes.

5. Have the boys and girls pray after you: "Thank You, Jesus, for allowing Your body to suffer and die for me." Then instruct them to eat the bread.

6. Have the children repeat, "Thank You, Jesus, for shedding Your blood for me." Then instruct them to drink the juice.

7. Sing a worship chorus.

Footwashing

Some of the most blessed services we've had in kids church have been when we've observed footwashing. It's a potent symbolic and spiritual act.

The Example

As with all the sacraments, Jesus provided the example in footwashing. Even though "Jesus knew that His hour had come that He should depart," Jesus' mind was not on Himself, but on His disciples, whom "He loved . . . to the end" (John 13:1 NKJV).

Without any explanation, Jesus "rose from supper and laid aside His garments, took a towel and girded Himself. After that, He poured water into a basin and began to wash the disciples' feet" (vv. 4-5 NKJV). Jesus even washed the filthy feet of Judas Iscariot, who would betray Him with a kiss only hours later!

The Meaning of Footwashing

Most obviously, footwashing is an act of humble service—the Master washing the disciples' feet, providing them a pattern of servanthood. If Jesus could wash their feet, they could wash one another's feet, for "a servant is not greater than his master" (v. 16 NKJV).

But footwashing has a deeper meaning which must be conveyed to children. As with the other sacraments, it is strongly connected with the atoning death of Jesus Christ.

When Peter said to Jesus, "You shall never wash my feet!", Jesus answered, "If I do not wash you, you have no part with Me" (v. 8 NKJV). Obviously, Jesus wasn't just talking about clean feet, but about a spiritual cleansing. Jesus went on to say, "He who is bathed needs only to wash his feet" (v. 10 NKJV).

In those days, a person who was otherwise clean could quickly have dirty feet because of wearing sandals on dusty streets. So when he entered a home, the first thing to do was to get his feet washed.

As Christians, we have been cleansed from sins—we have been made "completely clean" (v. 10) by the blood of Christ. But every day we must walk in a filthy world where temptation attacks our mind, body and soul. So footwashing reminds us that we need the same blood of Christ which saved us to keep us and cleanse us from the sin that abounds.

A Command and a Promise

The Command. Once you've helped children discover the meaning of footwashing, it's time to look at the command Jesus gave in John 13:14: "If I then, your Lord and Teacher, have washed your feet, you also ought to wash one another's feet" (NKJV).

Here are seven questions you can ask to explore this command:

1. Who is speaking in this verse? (Jesus Christ)
2. To whom is He speaking? (His disciples)
3. How was Jesus the disciples' "Teacher"? (He had taught them the Word of God.)

4. What does it mean to say Jesus is "Lord"? (He is the Master.)
5. Why would it be strange for the Lord and the Teacher to wash the feet of His students? (That was a servant's job. The disciples would have been expected to wash the Master's feet.)
6. Why do you suppose Jesus washed His disciples' feet? (He did it to show them His love; to teach them about His cleansing blood; to give them an example to follow.)
7. After He washed their feet, what did Jesus command them to do? (He told them to wash one another's feet.)

The Promise. After Jesus washed His disciples' feet and taught them about footwashing, He said, "If you know these things, blessed are you if you do them" (v. 17 NKJV).

Overcoming Obstacles

Before we can expect children to take part in footwashing, there are some practical concerns we should address. Let's look at answers to some questions kids might have:

Why should I let another person wash my feet? What's the point?

It is normal to have those kinds of feelings when you think about footwashing. However, it will probably help you to know that girls are separated from guys in foot-washing services.

The reason you should let someone else wash your feet is that Jesus has told us to wash one another's feet.

Washing someone else's feet is an old, old custom that went out when socks and shoes came in! It couldn't have any significance today.

We should participate in footwashing (1) because Jesus told us to, (2) to remind us of the cleansing power of Jesus' blood, (3) to show love to one another.

What kind of soap will we use? Will I have to bring a washcloth?

No soap and no washcloths are needed. You will not be scrubbing one another's feet.

Do we wash our feet before we come to church, or do we come with dirty feet?

People like to come to the service with clean feet. The point is not to actually scrub dirt off someone's toes! You can simply scoop handfuls of water over the person's feet and gently touch their feet.

What do I do while I wash someone else's feet—try to keep my mind on something else?

You should pray for this person as you wash his or her feet. Pray that your friend will love Jesus above all else and allow the blood of Jesus to keep cleansing his or her life. Pray that you and your friend will love each other as members of God's family.

I wouldn't be caught dead washing that *person's feet!*

One of the purposes of footwashing is to help us overcome wrong feelings toward others. If you humble yourself to wash the feet of someone you've not been getting along with, what might happen? (God would probably cause forgiveness and love to replace the bitter feelings.)

Don't forget that Jesus washed the feet of Judas!

Observing Footwashing

When observing footwashing with children, I've made it a special service in which older elementary-age kids participate. I take these steps:

1. Separate the boys from the girls.
2. Break each group into pairs.
3. Have adult leaders get into pairs.
4. Have the children take turns washing one another's feet and praying for each other.
5. Sing songs focusing on unity and the cleansing ministry of Christ.

When we celebrate footwashing with children, God blesses in a special way. Jesus keeps His promise to bless us for obeying Him.

Children Can Pray, Walk, and Live in the Spirit

Lance Colkmire

The Holy Spirit doesn't discriminate. Life in the Spirit is available to all regardless of social status, race, education . . . or age.

Revival Then

In the early years of the Church of God, the *Evangel* frequently contained testimonies of God's working in children's lives. Here are four examples:

- "There are about 150 members of the Church of God at Aricoma, West Virginia. About 30 children [have] received the Holy Ghost in the last four months. Hallelujah!" —Fannie Conley (July 2, 1921)

- "The Lord has wonderfully manifested Himself here (Charleston, Mississippi) this year. Many have been saved, sanctified and filled with the Holy Ghost. The sick have been healed. One little girl who had lost her voice was instantly healed when the saints prayed for her, and she went to the organ and sang and played."—E. Haynes (October 17, 1914)

- "My schoolmates persecute me but I mean to hold on to Jesus. Pray for my schoolmates. I love them and want to see them saved. I want to live a life that will be convincing to the children. I am a little girl only 11 years old but I know Jesus and He loves me. —Arzona Raynor, Omaha, Arkansas (March 13, 1920)

- "I received the Holy Ghost in the woods at children's prayer meeting. I love the Church of God and her teachings. Pray for us here at Bogalusa,

Louisiana, that many children will receive the Holy Ghost and come into the Church of God."—Minny Hathorne (April 16, 1921)

Scriptural Precedent

Those *Evangel* testimonies shouldn't surprise us, for they are consistent with Scripture.

- During a time when "there was no widespread revelation," the Holy Spirit spoke prophetically through a boy named Samuel (1 Sam. 3).

- When King Saul rebelled against God, the "the Spirit of the Lord came upon David"—the young shepherd who would become the next king (16:13, NKJV).

- God used the testimony of a servant girl to bring healing to a commanding officer who had leprosy (2 Kings 5).

- Jesus resurrected a 12-year-old girl (Mark 5:41-42), delivered a boy from an evil spirit (Matt. 17:14-18), and used a child's lunch to perform an awesome miracle (John 6:8-13).

- "This is what God had the prophet Joel say, 'When the last days come, I will give my Spirit to everyone'" (Acts 2:16-17 CEV).

- Peter preached, "Turn back to God! . . . Then you will be given the Holy Spirit. This promise is for you and your children. It is for everyone our Lord God will choose" (vv. 38-39 CEV).

What Is God Up To Today?

Here are five reasons I believe God wants to pour out His Spirit on our children today.

1. He promised to do it. And God always keeps His Word.

2. God loves children.

3. Like never before, our children need the infilling of the Holy Spirit. Satan is working through the media, secular schools, broken homes, and the erosion of Christian values in an unprecedented effort to capture our children. But God's Word promises, "When the enemy shall come in like a flood, the Spirit of the Lord shall lift up a standard against him" (Isa. 59:19).

4. There is something powerful about the praises of children. The psalmist wrote, "From the lips of children and infants you have ordained praise because of your enemies, to silence the foe and the avenger" (Ps. 8:2).

5. God wants His Spirit to flow through children. God wants to anoint children to pray, worship, and witness.

Teaching Children About the Holy Spirit

Understanding who the Holy Spirit is and what He does is a starting point for guiding children toward a Spirit-filled life.

Teach Who the Holy Spirit Is

He is God, coequal with God the Father and God the Son.

He is a spirit. Because of this . . .

- He is omnipresent—everywhere at the same time.
- Like the wind, we cannot see Him. But we can feel His presence, see His acts, and hear His voice (see John 3:8 and Acts 2:2).

He is a person. Because He loves us, we grieve Him when we disobey Him (Eph. 4:30).

He is holy. This means He is sinless, one-of-a-kind, and perfect.

The Bible is holy because the Spirit of God inspired its writing.

Teach What the Holy Spirit Does

1. He convicts us of sin and draws us to Jesus (John 16:8).
2. When we put our trust in Jesus, the Holy Spirit comes to live with us and in us (1 Cor. 6:19).
3. He guides the Christian (Rom. 8:14).
4. He produces spiritual fruit in the believer's life (Gal. 5:22-23).
5. He comforts believers (John 16:6-7).

When you tell the stories of the Old Testament, lift up the ministry of the Holy Spirit. For instance:

- The Holy Spirit helped to create the world (Gen. 1:1-2).
- The Spirit of God led the Hebrews by manifesting His presence through a cloud and a fire (Ex. 40:34-38).
- The judges (such as Samson, Judges 15:14) did their mighty deeds through the enablement of the Spirit.
- The Holy Spirit enabled people to prophesy (Num. 24:2-3; 1 Sam 19:19-24; 2 Chron. 15:1-2).
- The Holy Spirit gifted people to write (Jer. 30:2).
- Men and women in Old Testament times prophesied, sang, built, and performed miracles through the power of the Spirit.

Also teach about the Holy Spirit's ministry as recorded in the New Testament:

- Jesus was anointed and led by the Holy Spirit throughout His earthly ministry (Luke 4:1, 18)
- The Acts of the Apostles would better be named the "Acts of the Spirit," for that book is filled with stories about how the Spirit of God grew the church. For instance, you should teach how the gifts of the Spirit operated in the early church: sacrificial giving (2:45), hospitality (2:46), healing (3:1-10), miracles (5:12), martyrdom (7:51-60), evangelism (8:29-38), discernment (13:9-10), wisdom (15:13-21), preaching (20:3), and knowledge (27:23-26).

Help Children to Seek Sanctification

Teach your children that one of the works the Holy Spirit wants to do in their lives is sanctification—setting them apart from sin for His holy purpose. Focus on both aspects: (1) the Holy Spirit wants to deliver kids from sinful habits (2) so He can use them in special ways.

Explain that we are sanctified through the blood of Jesus (1 John 1:7), the Word of God (John 17:17), and the Spirit of God (1 Thess. 5:23).

Just as you periodically allow children the opportunity to receive Christ, so sometimes give altar calls in which children can pray to be sanctified. Teach them that while sanctification starts at a particular time, it is also an ongoing process.

Help Children Receive the Baptism in the Spirit

Start With the Need

The purpose of the baptism in the Spirit is to equip the believer with power for Christian living and Christian ministry. Tell the Bible stories of people, such as Simon Peter and Paul, whose lives were revolutionized after they were filled with the Spirit. Also, have people in your church testify to the children about what the baptism in the Spirit means to them.

Show Them How

First, teach that the baptism in the Spirit is a gift from God (Luke 11:11-13) offered to all believers (Acts 2:39).

Second, present three simple guidelines:

1. They must give themselves completely to God, holding back nothing.
2. They should begin to praise the Lord for the gift even before they receive it.
3. They should wait expectantly for the gift, receiving it by faith. Explain that the first sign of being filled with the Spirit will be when they speak in a language they have never learned. They will not understand the words, but God will. The words will glorify God and fill the believer with joy.

Focus on Life in the Spirit

We Pentecostals have often been guilty of focusing on receiving the baptism without emphasizing how the baptism should change one's life. We should repeatedly teach the following truths to our children:

1. We are to "keep on being filled with the Spirit," which is the meaning of Ephesians 5:18. This happens when we keep on yielding ourselves to the Holy Spirit.
2. We are to "walk in the Spirit" (Gal. 5:16, 26). We are to listen to His voice and obey Him day by day.
3. We are to allow the fruit of the Spirit to grow in our lives (Gal. 5:22-23).
4. We are to allow speaking in tongues to be an ongoing part of our prayer lives (1 Cor. 14:18).
5. We are to serve God through the gifts the Holy Spirit gives us (1 Cor. 12).
6. We are to allow the Holy Spirit to make us into a church of friends loving each other and working in harmony (Acts 2:42-47).

Follow Nehemiah's Example

God wants to move mightily among the children in every church.

You can help make it happen by following the example of Nehemiah.

1. *Discern the need.* Nehemiah, a Jew living in Persia, received a full report on the condition of Jerusalem—the people were "in great trouble and disgrace," the wall around the city was "broken down," and its gates had been burned (Neh. 1:3).

   Here's the full report on children—Satan's strategy against them is to steal, kill and destroy (John 10:10).

2. *Repent.* Nehemiah repented of his personal sins and the sins of Israel. Today, you must repent of your personal sins and the sins of your church. You must be revived if you want God to use you to help bring about revival.

3. *Intercede.* Nehemiah said, "For some days I mourned and fasted and prayed before the God of heaven" (Neh. 1:4).

   God is looking for intercessors who will pray and fast on behalf of children. Will you intercede for your kids?

4. *Spread the vision.* When Nehemiah arrived in Jerusalem, he said to the Jews, "Come, let us rebuild the wall of Jerusalem, and we will no longer be in disgrace" (v. 17).

   Your vision for revival needs to be shared with church leaders who will help you bear the burden.

5. *Have a strategy.* The Jews separated to work on each section of the wall all at once. Everyone from administrative officials to officials' daughters took part in the demanding work. A successful strategy for bringing revival to children is likewise a team effort—ministry to children should be in focus in children's church, in corporate worship, and in the home.

6. *Fight the enemy.* When Nehemiah's enemies "heard that the repairs to Jerusalem's walls had gone ahead and that the gaps were being closed, they were very angry. They all plotted together to come and fight against Jerusalem" (4:7-8).

   Satan hates revival and he despises children; so be ready for his attack.

7. *Persevere.* When the plot was discovered, Nehemiah prayed first. Then he equipped half of his men with weapons while the other half kept working (4:9, 16). You will persevere by continuing to pray, fast, and work.

8. *Let God do it!* When the wall was finished in only 52 days, Jerusalem's enemies "were very disheartened . . . for they perceived that this work was done by God" (6:16 NKJV). When the Holy Spirit brings revival, you will know it—for He will be accomplish things only He can accomplish. Expect to be amazed!

9. *Teach the Word.* After the wall was completed, "all the people assembled as one man" (8:1). Thirteen Levites "read from the Book of the Law of God, making it clear and giving the meaning so that the people could understand what was being read" (v. 8).

Teaching God's Word to children will make them hungry for God; as revival takes place, the Word will establish them in Christ; and as they go forth to worship and minister, the Word will show them how to walk in the Spirit.

20
Helping Kids Find, Develop, and Use Their Gifts

Lynn Miller

There are a number of books that touch briefly on the topic of children utilizing spiritual gifts. The majority of these books try to convince readers that children do have the capacity to receive spiritual gifts and should be allowed to use them. You and I already know children are capable of ministering through spiritual gifts, so let's dive right into the "how to's" of gift discovery and implementation.

To discover their spiritual gifts, many people try to use the gift-testing exercises located in those same books I just mentioned. This works well for adults, but usually fails miserably when applied to children. The reason these exercises are faulty is that they are based on a person's prior experiences. The books ask questions that only experienced adults would know how to answer, such as "Have you ever felt fulfilled after teaching a lesson?" or "When you learn about a person's financial need, do you feel compelled to help them?" How would a child who's never taught a lesson or received a paycheck be able to answer such questions? The answer is, he or she won't.

Children are still in the discovery stage of life. Every new event brings with it a life lesson or discovery of some sort. It is our task as leaders to offer children the experiences they need in order to help them determine what their spiritual gifts are.

God instills both talents and gifts in children. Talents are natural abilities. Gifts are revealed when the child's actions meet with supernatural designs to bring God glory. One year I attended a week-long camp meeting. On the first evening a very talented young girl sang a solo. Her voice was beautiful and she hit every note perfectly. Everyone applauded when she was done. The girl's younger sister sang a solo on the fourth evening. The younger girl didn't have as much musical talent as her sister and her voice cracked twice during the song. However, her worship was so beautiful that the entire congregation began singing along with her. When the solo was over, there was no applause because everyone was standing, hands raised in the air, worshipping God. The girl quietly put down the microphone and walked off the platform while the congregation continued to sing praises to God. The difference between the two girls was simple: the older was talented and the younger was gifted.

Helping children discover and develop the gifts God has placed within them requires three things: directed conversations, observation and follow-through.

Directed Conversations

Asking specific questions of the child, their parents and other family members can help you determine where to begin in assessing your students. Before getting into the details of using directed conversations, note that parents can be a tremendous help and at times a hindrance in determining spiritual gifts. This is because they are biased towards their children. They tend to think their children are good at everything. A parent who believes their child is perfect in every way will not be of much help in telling you where a child may actually excel. There are also times when parents have preconceived ideas about where a spiritual gift may direct their child's life. A parent can easily dismiss the gift if they feel it might lead their child on a difficult path. Although these situations are not the norm, you should be aware that this kind of parental behavior does exist.

Directed conversations will happen naturally as you begin talking with parents. These conversations do not have to be forced or scheduled. Learn to listen to both the positive and negative things that families say. Pay attention when parents brag on their children—they may be telling you about a gift that is already active in the child's life.

A parent stopped me in the hallway one day to tell me how proud they were of their son, Jacob. He had decided that, for his birthday, the children should bring adult-sized gloves and scarves instead of bringing presents for him. After the party, he donated the items to the local homeless shelter. Through listening to the parent, I recognized the gift of giving actively working in Jacob's life. Later, when I asked him if he'd like to testify about the event in children's worship, he declined. His exact words were, "I didn't do it so that others would find out and be proud of me." This child already understood Jesus' teaching, "When you give to the needy, do not let your left hand know what your right hand is doing" (Matt. 6:3).

Listening to a parent's negative comments may give insight about a child as well. When a parent expresses concern about their child's church experience, the automatic tendency of a leader is to get defensive. Instead the leader should seize the moment and turn it into a directed conversation. Rather than receiving it as a complaint, the leader should hear a cry for help.

One mother told a children's leader, "I'm having a difficult time getting Bailey to come to children's worship. She loves the teacher, but she doesn't enjoy kids church."

"Has Bailey mentioned why she doesn't like coming to kids church?" the leader asked.

"No."

"Has this been a sudden change in Bailey's behavior?"

"No. It's been gradual. She never complained when her sister was with her. Now that her sister has moved up, she's become disinterested."

(The leader could have ended the conversation at this moment and easily explained away the behavior as separation anxiety. Instead, she chose to direct the conversation further and try to find out more about Bailey.)

"I'm sure Bailey was more comfortable with her older sister around," the leader empathized. "That is completely understandable. I'd like to get Bailey comfortable in class without her sister. Has she mentioned anything that she does like about children's worship?"

"She said something the other day about the kids who help with the check-in. And she's mentioned the offering contest. She said it is fun."

"Has she ever been asked to help with the check-in?"

"I don't think so."

"Does she like to help you around the house?"

"Oh, yes! Bailey loves to help with housework. Can you believe she'll even help clean the bathroom? She's my little sweetheart!"

"Would it be okay with you if I asked Bailey to leave her Sunday school class 10 minutes early next week and help me with the check-in process?"

"I guess so. Do you think helping will make her want to be in children's worship more?"

"I don't know," the leader answered honestly. "I'll try to find ways to involve Bailey in serving the next three weeks. Let's talk in a month and see how she's doing."

Bailey became a junior helper in kids church. She quickly began serving in other areas of ministry and even took on the jobs that other children cringed at doing. Once she realized her help was of value, she enjoyed coming to the house of God. Bailey has the gift of service.

Having a directed conversation with a parent will give insight about the child that the leader would never have otherwise. A list of sample questions and the possible gifts that could coincide with a "yes" answer are these:

- Has the child ever given away a new toy? (giving)
- Does the child enjoy making new friends, no matter what the age, race or gender? (hospitality)
- Does the child like to help younger family members? (teaching)
- Do other children follow this child's ideas? (administration)
- Does the child offer to help with chores? (service)
- Does the child pray for the needs of others and expect immediate healing? (faith)
- Does the child have a keen sense of right and wrong? (discernment)
- Is the child compassionate when others are hurting? (mercy)

Children usually assume they are gifted in the area of life they enjoy most. If this were the case, most children would be professional ice-cream tasters or video-game players. Thankfully God has gifted His children according to His purpose, not their opinions. Directed conversations will help leaders and parents go deeper than opinions and try to discover true giftedness.

Observation

Observing children in ministry is another way to learn about their giftedness. In order to see a spiritual gift in action, events must be planned which will allow the spiritual gift to function. For example, altar calls and child-led lessons can take place during the worship service. Outreach and service projects will also give the leader an opportunity to witness the children's gifts. The leader who wants the gifts of the Spirit active in their ministry must do the work needed to unearth them.

To find intercessors, the leader could plan altar calls that encourage children to pray for a specific need. Follow these simple steps to observe children who pray for others.

1. After your message, give an altar call as you normally would.
2. Before praying for those who respond to the altar call, ask the children who are Spirit-filled and have not come forward to stand behind the children in the altar.
3. As you pray, make sure to take notice of who is praying intensely for others. If a child is moving from person to person, laying hands on them but not praying for them, quietly send the child back to their seat. That is a distraction. If a child is playing with another child's hair or clothing,

gently hold his or her hand still and whisper, "Pray for them; don't play with them." Failing to use proper etiquette does not mean a child is not interceding. There may just be a need for training.

4. Observe which children continue praying until the last child finishes praying. These are the intercessors.

5. Continue this process for several weeks. Intercession is not a gift that comes and goes. The children who are so gifted will regularly be active in prayer times.

Discovering the teaching gift is a different process altogether. A leader who is honestly looking for those who are set apart to teach and preach must be willing to do something very difficult—release some personal ministry time to the children. Allowing children the opportunity to get in front of others and lead a lesson takes courage for both the child and the leader.

1. Ask the Lord to reveal the children who are faithful to Him. Whenever a child comes to mind, contact that child. Ask if they would be interested in teaching a short lesson. If the child agrees, say you will contact their parents to find out what dates they will definitely be present.

2. Once a date is set, get the lesson information to the child. The information should include three things: the Bible story for the day, the Scripture verse, and the main point. Give the child liberty to pick which one he or she would like to teach on. Instruct the child to seek God for help. Encourage the child's family to help with ideas as well. Families are good practice audiences too.

3. Commit to praying for the child every day until he or she teaches.

4. Contact the child a few days before the lesson to find out if help is needed and to confirm the date.

5. Prior to the service, place the child's name on the lesson outline. Show the child the outline when they arrive so they will know when it's their turn.

6. While the child is teaching, stand close by. This will allow you to be ready to help in any way.

7. After the child is finished, briefly clarify any points that may have been vague, and then publicly compliment the child.

Teachers love to impart knowledge. If the child has the gift of teaching, he or she will present a well-prepared lesson with a clear message. The lesson does not have to be long to be powerful, nor does the speech have to eloquent to be understood.

Last year I asked Danny to teach a lesson about keeping Christ in Christmas. He prepared fervently for three weeks. When he showed up to teach he had no supplies, no props, and no outline. This made me a little nervous, but I brought the 10-year-old forward anyway. He taught for 20 minutes, incorporating the other students in his lesson. Children and adults alike listened intently to him and received insight from God. It was an amazing moment to witness the spiritual gift of teaching in action for the first time in Danny's life.

Discovering those who have the gift of preaching occurs in a similar manner. When a child is gifted to preach, he or she will try to find ways to encourage others to act on the lesson. An example of this was when Ben taught on obedience. On his appointed day, he was armed with two pages of notes and spoke for over 25 minutes. He used an object lesson, told a Bible story, and gave an altar call. Six children were filled with the Spirit! I did not preach that day because Ben, who had only been asked to teach an object lesson, had preached my sermon! God is not concerned about the age of His messenger—He just wants his message delivered.

Other gifts—such as word of knowledge, discernment, administration, prophecy, and evangelism—can be found among children as well. A third grader was asked to teach a lesson about world missions. She told a quick story about a missionary. Then she said, "God told me to pray for you today. He is going to tell some of you where you are going to be missionaries." She prayed over the children and then asked individuals to stand if God had spoken to them directly. Three children stood with assurance and gave the names of the countries where God told them they would minister. Within four years, all three of those children had been on short-term mission trips and had begun to prepare themselves for mission work. In her childlike manner, the third-grader displayed the gift of knowledge. Remember, gifts are revealed when the child's actions meet with supernatural designs to bring God glory.

Administration is revealed when a child who is serving in some way begins to organize that area of ministry. Administration comes forth when the child approaches the leader with new methods to better the ministry or when they begin directing others who are serving with them. The leader will know if it is truly a gift and not just bossiness when the child's ideas are workable and those around them gladly complete the tasks the child asks of them.

Prophecy is not a gift that can be planned for. God sends His prophecies whenever and to whomever He chooses. When it happens in a child's life, the leader should encourage the child to write down everything that God has spoken. A few years ago a church in our area had a prayer walk on their campus. One child tagged along with his mother for the walk. As they prayed over each room, they came to one that was full of expensive equipment. The little boy stopped and cried out, "Robbers, Mommy! Robbers! I see robbers!" The mother and other leaders assured him there were no robbers in the church. The boy gradually settled down and the prayer walk continued. That night the church was broken into and the room where the little boy had prophesied was cleaned out by the thieves.

Every time God uses a child to prophesy, 2 Peter 1:21 is lived out: "For prophecy never had its origin in the will of man, but men spoke from God as they were carried along by the Holy Spirit."

Continued Training

Commit yourself to training the children who have demonstrated spiritual gifts. Children must understand the proper function of the gift God has entrusted to them. Exercising the gifts and being held accountable for how they are used will help children develop into mature Christians. Children who are teachers and preachers should be given multiple opportunities to minister and should be instructed/corrected by adults when needed. If a child can administrate, trust them with responsibility according to their level of ability. Givers can help with service projects and offering lessons. Intercessors need the freedom to pray in the altars and take part in prayer chains. Those with faith should regularly be called upon to pray. Every children's ministry director is looking for more workers. There are already many young ones in their classes, just waiting to be mobilized!

In following through with spiritual-gift training, make sure to keep in contact with the child's family. Godly parents want to be involved in their child's spiritual development. The family will notice specific activity taking place in the home or school environment that will give you updates about the child's growth. Communication between the child's family and church leaders is vital when tailoring the training to meet each child's unique needs.

Ask God to reveal ways you can follow through with those who have exhibited spiritual gifts. The more your eyes are opened to what God is doing through his children, the more "His kingdom [will] come [and] his will be done, on earth as it is in heaven" (Matt. 6:10).

CHILDREN LEADING CHILDREN

Kashif Andrew Graham

If anyone has ministered to a group of inner-city teens or children, you know that getting them to cooperate can be quite difficult. However, this task is not impossible. The prophetic words of Isaiah 11:6—"a little child will lead them"—can help.

It was the dead of summer—the point in July when all you can think about is how to get cool. The midsummer heat tends to sap one's energy and breed short-temperedness. On top of it all, I was on a team ministering to 60-plus inner-city youth for the first time at a Vacation Bible School in New York.

The program started with a number of fights among a few students. Amidst our sing-alongs and the lavishly adorned sanctuary, those we were serving gave little recognition of our efforts. In the moment, it felt that this program would be short-lived.

My position of service gave me opportunities to observe particular activities each night. I noticed a certain youth—very overweight, and not by any means silent. He would walk the hallways with other students and spew out negative comments in their direction. In return, they would retort with something harsher. I soon realized that this student was struggling with self-esteem issues and had no idea how to handle them.

As we were closing out on a particular night, and getting the kids loaded into the church van, I noticed this young man took a prime seat up front next to the driver, who was my aunt. I patted his shoulder through the window, "Hey, Champ! I'm trusting you to take care of my aunt for me. Can you do that?" He nodded.

From that point on, I perceived a shift in our relationship. Each time I would see him, he would receive a greeting like "How's it going, Champ?" or "Hey, Champ!" He would respond positively, even if it was just a small nod.

Eventually, I began to realize the younger children were modeling their behavior after him. Because he was from their community, he influenced them. In fact, there were many times I would try to correct a student, and he or she would not comply. However, if I encouraged "Champ" to do the right thing, he would change his behavior and reprimand the others in return. *Children listen to other children.*

I recognized it is acceptable to employ children in children's ministry. In doing this, we will help to craft leaders. Youth do not have to only be *future* leaders, but they can also be *today's leaders.*

Of course, this comes with a disclaimer. The children we utilize in ministry are also subject to discipline as well. This is part of what makes them leaders. They are also taught to respect rules in their places of leadership—being a helper does not exempt a student from the rules at hand. Rather, student-leaders are encouraged to model leadership through cooperation and respect.

I also believe in reminding the children who are helping their peers that they will not be allowed to continue leading if they choose to model poor behavior. Meanwhile, I support rewarding leadership through small tokens and words of affirmation.

Finally, to prevent students from being overwhelmed with rules and regulations, I like to have them repeat: "Fun, but safety first." This keeps our mission in check, and helps students to remember that we want them to have fun while learning.

To recap:

1. It's good to have children involved in leading your VBS or other children's ministry activity.

2. Remind children who help you lead that they are examples and not above the rules.
3. Give out small tokens of appreciation and/or words of affirmation for exemplary leadership.
4. Always look for ways to affirm students.
5. Children can be leaders *today*.

Expecting God to Show Up in Our Children's Worship Service

Lynn Miller

I was filled with the Holy Spirit and then prayed for a girl, and she spoke in tongues!"

Laney's excitement bubbled out as she bounced up and down in front of her father. The father looked up at me, saw my affirming head nod, and then knelt to hug Laney as his eyes swelled with tears. He understood the value of that moment. When a child experiences God's grace and power, they are solidified in Him and all of the lives surrounding them are influenced for Christ. A supernatural children's service impacts the entire church body.

Many believe that a *supernatural move* of the Holy Spirit cannot be planned. They think God *shows up* whenever He wants and only those who are spiritually aware will *flow with the Spirit* and experience the *presence of God*. (Whew! That is a whole lot of Pentecostal words used to describe our ineffective worship services!) Since it is believed that we cannot prepare for when God *moves*, the idea of planning a supernatural service seems a bit contrived. However, there are many biblical accounts where the opposite is proven true.

Elijah literally *planned* for fire to fall from heaven. . . . Elisha gave specific *instructions* for Naaman to be completely healed from leprosy. . . . Mary *gathered* servants at a wedding and *directed* them to follow through with whatever Jesus instructed.

In each Biblical example, the leaders were *preparing* for a supernatural event. Likewise, we can prepare for a supernatural event in our children's services. Just as school lessons can be organized to teach history to a child, spiritual lessons can be prepared to teach children how to function in the Holy Spirit. Some may view a supernatural expectant lesson to be one that intentionally stirs up emotions. Let's stop right here and clarify—we cannot teach children how to speak in tongues, heal others, or prophesy! Those are God's gifts to them. Our task is to teach them how to use the spiritual gift appropriately, once bestowed.

Leaders, functioning as the Father's representatives, should not be afraid to prepare lessons and hands-on training for the children. Listed below are several suggestions on how to prepare a service so children can experience God's incredible power and learn to minister to one another. Some of these ideas, if thoughtfully implemented, will provide immediate results. Others must be consistently integrated into the service to allow for training, correction, and experiential wisdom to develop.

Move the message and prayer time to the middle of the service.

Just because altar calls are traditionally held at the end of the service does not mean they should be. There are many reasons to move the message to the middle of service, and here are two common examples: (1) When two friends plan to bombard their parents after church, asking to spend the afternoon together, they are going to concentrate on their exit strategy when they sense the service is ending. (2) If a parent has to leave for work and must exit fifteen minutes before the church service ends, they are going to pick up their child early.

Rather than being frustrated that children won't linger at the altar or complaining that a parent snatches their child up while he or she is still praying, move the prayer time. Object lessons, skits, star student awards, and review games can still take place after the message.

Plan praise songs to engage the mind and body, preparing both for the Word.

It is important for children to be mentally and physically engaged when the message and prayer time take place. When a boy is singing praise songs, he is actively participating in the service. Capturing the attention of his heart, mind, and hands is crucial to the service's outcome. An attentive eight-year-old is a rare thing. A boy who has lifted his hands in worship and then, twelve minutes later, anxiously places those hands on a friend who is praying for boldness will seek God with expectancy. On the contrary, a boy who just finished playing marshmallow dodgeball and then sits through a twelve-minute message will be anxious to show his friend the marshmallow he tucked in his pocket while the rest of the kids go pray at the altar. The proper placement of praise songs is crucial to a supernatural service.

Don't dawdle.

Children tend to be more responsive to God's Word than adults. This is one of the many advantages of ministering to children! Whenever children hear of something they should be doing or could be doing, they want to experience it immediately. Children cannot tolerate a two-chapter, three-point sermon.

We have all experienced the camp speaker who thought the more wisdom he or she imparted, the greater the move of God would be. Then we see the opposite effect: an hour-long message, which left children disinterested, and mentally and physically wandering around. There is no need to belabor the point. For example, when teaching about God's ability to heal the sick: creatively tell the Bible story, teach a Scripture verse, share a testimony, and then maximize on children's eagerness and get them to ministering!

Accept that a child's faith is strong.

Children have no problem believing in spiritual things. When a child hears that Cornelius and his household were filled with the Holy Spirit, they believe they can be filled too. Their lack of doubt about whether or not they are worthy to be baptized in the Holy Spirit is a beautiful thing. Their excitement over receiving the baptism outweighs any reservations they may have about the experience.

I have seen hundreds of children filled with the power of the Holy Spirit by simply teaching a Scripture verse (such as John 20:22; Acts 2:4; Mark 1:8; or John 3:34), sharing a Bible example and contemporary story about someone being filled with the Spirit, and then inviting kids to prayerfully ask God for this gift.

Regularly invite children to the altar.

Learning to pray—admitting sin (confessing), apologizing (asking forgiveness), and listening (waiting on God)—is a process. Communication with God is learned through example and repetition. To help children become accustomed to praying in the altar, provide the opportunity for them to pray about whatever is being taught on during the service. If the lesson is on *obedience*, children can pray for obedient hearts. If the lesson is on *hate*, children should pray for their enemies. Regularly bringing children forward for prayer opens a child's spiritual sensitivity level. As children grow more comfortable praying at the altar, they will be less self-conscious about bringing their needs to the Lord and will get bolder in praying for others.

Provide two altar calls.

Since salvation is the most important of all the supernatural occurrences, it is imperative that we regularly provide an opportunity for children to receive Christ as Savior. Even if salvation is not the lesson emphasis, there may be a child present who recognizes his or her need of a Savior. For example, a lesson on *covetousness* could reveal a heart issue requiring more than a plea for help from the Father; it could disclose the fact that the child needs to be saved by a loving God who will clean the heart and make it new! One prayer time set aside for those who recognize their need of salvation can easily precede a prayer time for the believers who struggle with covetousness and need the Holy Spirit's power to help them overcome this temptation.

Allow children to minister as the Spirit enables them.

When a child is filled with the Spirit, he or she has the authority of God within to function as a representative for Him. We should help children become fellow representatives for Christ, allowing them to minister as God directs them. Creating a structured portion of the service where children learn to function as such is crucial. Often, altar calls are brought to a close prior to children ministering, due to the leader's lack of knowledge of how to release them into action. Remember, we *can* plan for salvations, healings, words of knowledge, and so on, because we know God functions in those ways and delights in doing so in our midst. A few intentional methods for allowing children to minister are suggested here.

- Call the children forward who need healing, or who want to stand in the place of someone who needs healing, and let the other children gather around to pray for them. It may seem that this is too obvious of an example to mention. However, when the children are invited to corporately agree ("yes, Lord" and "amen") as one child at a time prays out loud for healing, unity is created. We have witnessed deaf ears healed, scoliosis backs straightened, visible viruses instantly healed, and broken bones fused . . . and with each healing our faith increases!

- Anoint children with oil and pray for God's specific direction in their lives, and then send them to pray in small groups. Allow children to share what God speaks to them. I have seen missionaries, pastors, professors, and others set on a path for ministry in this manner.

- Invite those who are fearful (of the dark, death, being robbed, and so on) to the altar. Allow Spirit-filled-children to pray individually with them and share personal stories of God's ability to bring peace. One parent sent a thank-you note to the child who ministered to their son in the altar. The son had been having nightmares, but after his friend shared a story of God's light and prayed with him, the nightmares stopped.

- During prayer time, let Spirit-filled intercessors know that they may speak to the one they are praying for, but only if their words are a message from the Lord. Clarify by teaching children, "A *word from the Lord* is a message God wants the person to hear in human voice, but the human giving it wouldn't have any way of knowing the message unless it came from God." Many times the message may not mean much to the giver, but the one receiving knows exactly what it means and will be thankful God sent the message to them.

I've seen a child tell one girl that she was to forgive her father because he was coming home. The girl learned the next day that her incarcerated father (a fact the message giver was not aware of) had been miraculously released and was coming home. Another child was told, "You are pure. No matter what, God sees you as pure." The message giver had no idea that the child had been molested.

During directed prayer times, God invariably provides the ministering children with a keen focus. It still bewilders me when a hyperactive child will sit quietly, praying for another child and periodically lean forward to gently whisper, "God hears you. Keep your heart on Jesus."

Perform exciting events prior to the message and prayer time.

One example is our monthly Birthday Sunday. Every child gets a cupcake while the group sings the birthday song. This is done well before the message time. Why? When children know an exciting event will take place, they cannot concentrate on the moment at hand. The "Is it time?" and "When will we . . . ?" questions will plague them (and you!) until that event takes place. A children's service should have exciting elements built in, but waiting until the end of the service to experience them can create a distraction during the teaching times.

Instruct children while in prayer time.

Although prayer is communication between God and the soul seeking Him, learning how to stay focused and intercede for others can require specific instruction.

- Praying individually is easy at first, but less than three minutes into prayer, a child's eyes will pop open with intrigue about what is happening nearby. Curiosity is normal; it does not mean the child is done seeking God. Gently asking if he or she is done praying will help them to decide if they want to refocus or return to their seat. If a child chooses to refocus, ask him or her specifically what they are praying for and begin praying alongside of them for those specific requests. Call another child forward to help pray for them.

- *Interceding* is praying on behalf of another person. A child suddenly "laying hands" on another child during prayer generally creates more of a distraction than an encouragement. This can be avoided by instructing children to lightly place one hand on their friend's shoulder or upper back. Instruct them to not play with the child's clothing or hair and not to rub or tickle the child. Quickly remove children who are a physical distraction.

- When children are no longer praying but looking around or talking to others, send them back to their chairs. It is not wrong to tell children to leave the altar if they are not participating. As their prayer maturity increases, their time at the altar will increase as well.

Allow for different prayer times.

Not all prayers are said or answered in unison. When it is obvious that the majority of the children are done, yet one or more are earnestly praying, it is time to move one group or the other. Depending on the circumstance, you may move the praying children to a quieter location or you can dismiss the larger group to a different activity. If the praying children are truly communicating with God, moving will not shut it down.

One Sunday, a boy was praying very quietly, but I could tell he was repeating something. When his small group had been relocated and the distractions were removed, he felt comfortable enough to speak up and we realized he was prophesying. His words were written down, and two months later the prophecy was fulfilled. The point is, do not be afraid of movement during prayer time.

Seek the Lord for Each Service

Planning a supernatural service can be done whether curriculum is used or you write your own lessons. The most important thing you can do is inwardly prepare your heart to lead others into the presence of the Lord and ask God for discernment on how to direct the service.

Plan with faith. . . . Expect the supernatural. . . . God will show up.

22 Let the Children Praise Him!

Beth Barnes & Lance Colkmire

As children of God, we were created to praise, worship and glorify Him. Psalm 150:6 says, "Let everything that hath breath, praise the Lord." The key word in this verse is *everything*, which includes kids.

In Psalm 148:12-13, children are commanded to praise the Lord: "Both young men and maidens; old men and children. Let them praise the name of the Lord, for His name alone is exalted; His glory is above the earth and heaven" (NKJV).

There is power in the praises of children! David declared, "Out of the mouths of children and infants, you have ordained praise because of your enemies, to silence the foe and the avenger" (Ps. 8:2).

Hosanna!

When Jesus rode into Jerusalem on what we now refer to as Palm Sunday, "a very great multitude spread their clothes on the road; others cut down branches from the trees and spread them on the road. Then the multitudes . . . cried out, saying, 'Hosanna to the Son of David! Blessed is He who comes in the name of the Lord!'" (Matt. 21:8-9 NKJV).

No doubt children were among that Palm Sunday throng. They watched parents and grandparents shout hosannas, wave palm branches, and lay down their cloaks . . . and surely the boys and girls joined in.

Once Jesus entered the city gates, He went directly to His Father's house—the Temple. There the blind and the lame came to Jesus, and He healed them.

Children followed Jesus into the Temple and kept shouting, "Hosanna to the Son of David" (v. 15).

Rather than worshiping Jesus as the Christ as He healed the helpless, the chief priests and teachers of the Law were indignant! They were furious because of the miracles and because of the children's praises. (The children knew more than the leaders did!)

The religious leaders asked Jesus, "Do you hear what these children are saying?" Jesus replied, "Yes, have you never read, 'From the lips of children and infants you have ordained praise'?" (v. 16).

There are several things we can learn about children and worship from this dramatic passage:

- Children need adult role models who will teach them (by word and deed) how to worship.
- Children will worship God if provided the opportunity.
- There are a variety of ways children can praise God: shouting praises, waving their arms, and laying down something important are among them.
- Jesus has ordained the praises of children, and their praises can indeed silence the enemies of God.

Let's explore each of these four truths.

We Must Model Worship Before Children

Ideally, worship will be modeled before children from the beginning of their child's life.

Worship at Home

Worship should begin at home. We should encourage Christian parents to teach their kids to worship in daily living. Parents who render praise to God in the good times and in the bad will teach their children true praise. This is acting in obedience to the scripture, "In everything give thanks" (1 Thess. 5:18).

There is no more potent example than parents who "walk the walk" and "talk the talk" at home and then enter into worship at church. On the other hand, it damages children spiritually when a parent shouts praises at church but rants and raves at home. We must convey to parents how their worship example is molding their kids.

I'll never forget sitting behind little Larry at church one Sunday. People around the church were lifting their hands in worship, and Larry did the same. But when he looked over at his father and saw that his dad's hand was not lifted, the boy yanked his hand down. What a sermon!

"From the Mouths of Infants"

The nursery is where the love of Jesus is taught for the first time at church. What a privilege to be the first teacher in the church to tell a child, "Jesus loves you"! The nursery teacher can minister to babies by gathering them around her as she lifts praises to God.

Also, soft worship music can be played in the nursery. Recordings of Christian lullabies are a good choice.

In the Classroom

Teachers should teach that worship is showing respect to Jesus. Jesus is worthy of our respect and praise because of who He is. We should inspire kids to get excited about who Jesus is.

Teachers can help children develop an attitude of gratitude by setting aside time in class each week to give thanks to God. When a request the class has been praying about is answered, the teacher and the students should offer thanks together.

We Must Provide Children Opportunities to Worship

Praise and worship is not hard when the Holy Spirit touches a child's heart. We encourage kids to worship when we provide the time, the place, and the example.

Making Christ Central

Worship should be a central part of kids church. However, we can get so caught up with the "bells and whistles" that we fail to give worship (and Christ!) their rightful place.

The Lord Jesus must be the main focus if we want to motivate kids to make church attendance a lifelong habit. Jesus said, "I, when I am lifted up from the earth, will draw all men to myself" (John 12:32).

How do we lift up Christ in kids church, thereby motivating children to worship?

1. Teach who God is. Children need to know God as Paul describes Him in Ephesians 3:20: "He who is able to do immeasurably more than all we ask or imagine, according to his power that is at work within us." This means recognizing (1) He is the all-powerful, all-knowing, ever-present One who is "immeasurably" greater than we can imagine, (2) yet He is a personal God of love who desires to "work in us."

   An excellent scripture to use in portraying God in this manner is Isaiah 9:6: "His name shall be called Wonderful, Counselor, the mighty God, the everlasting Father, the Prince of Peace." You could use each of these names in teaching a series about who God is. The following Biblical accounts work well:

- Wonderful—the raising of Lazarus (John 11)
- Counselor—Jesus ministers to a Samaritan woman (John 4)
- The mighty God—the Creation (Genesis 1)
- The Prince of Peace—Jesus stills a storm (Luke 8:22-25)
- The everlasting Father—the prodigal son (Luke 15:11-32).

When kids begin to comprehend who God is and what He does, they will know why He is deserving of all praise.

2. Teach who we are. Kids need to see themselves as God sees them—as His creation, made to bring glory to His name. "You are worthy, our Lord and God, to receive glory and honor and power, for you created all things, and by your will they were created and have their being" (Rev. 4:11).

Creating an Atmosphere

Music sets the atmosphere. You can play uplifting songs as the kids enter the room. Use icebreaker songs or action songs. Your worship should also include Scripture songs, which puts the Word of God in children's mouths and hearts.

Make your song service come alive by using live music, DVD's, special singers, and a praise-and-worship team. Set aside a special time during your children's church service to sing worship songs. Close your eyes and focus on Jesus.

Worship at the Altar

Play soft worship music during the altar service. This helps kids focus their attention on God.

Praising God during the altar service teaches kids to praise and rejoice for what God is going to do in their lives. Teach kids to put their petitions before God and praise Him for the answer.

Jesus can do more in 30 seconds at an altar than a children's pastor can do in a year. Don't be afraid to let the Holy Spirit move in your children's church. Instead, be the example, letting the Holy Spirit work through you.

We Should Teach Children Various Expressions of Worship

As integral as singing is to worship, it is not the only scriptural way to praise. Unfortunately, though, that is the message we are conveying if we do not show children how to worship in other ways. And what impression does that give to children who do not like to sing—that they cannot worship?

In children's worship, we should encourage kids to worship in the following ways:

- Lifting hands as a sign of surrender to God (Ps. 134:2)
- Clapping hands as a joyous expression of praise (47:1)

- Shouting praise as a worshipful response to the joy God has given us (100:1)
- Kneeling before the Lord in honor of His greatness (95:6)
- Reading the Word of God and meditating on it (119:15)
- Giving an offering unto the Lord (2 Cor. 9:7)
- Being silent before the Lord (Hab. 2:20)
- Eating the Lord's Supper (1 Cor. 11:26).

Praise Breaks
One of the easiest ways to involve kids in praise is to have praise breaks during your services. During a praise break, kids close their eyes, stand, raise their hands and praise God out loud for 15 seconds. As the kids continue to praise in this way on a regular basis, it will become more comfortable and meaningful.

Testimonies
Give kids a chance to tell what God has done for them—yes, let them testify. You can do this by passing around a bean bag—the one holding the bean bag testifies, then it is passed on. The child praises God for something specific He has done in their life.

Worship Statements
Have the children repeat a praise after you, personalizing it to make it their own. For instance, "Jesus, _____ (child's name) loves You."

Personalizing Scripture
For instance, "The joy of the Lord is Todd's strength." Or, "Greater is he that is in Kristy than he that is in the world."

Jesus Has Ordained the Praises of Children
Children bring glory to God when they offer the Lord what is rightfully His. That is *worship* as defined in Romans 12:1: "When you offer your bodies to God, you are worshiping him" (NIRV).

Their Hearts
Someone said, "You can sing until you are blue in the face, but if it doesn't come from the heart, it isn't praise." We must teach children that the mechanics of worship (lifting hands, singing, kneeling, etc.) are meaningless unless they have accepted Jesus as their Savior. As Jesus said, "True worshipers will worship the Father in Spirit and truth" (John 4:23 NKJV).

Their Obedience

"We are his people, the sheep of his pasture" (Ps. 100:3), so we are to follow the Good Shepherd in obedience. In fact, genuine Sunday worship can take place only if the children are glorifying God in daily living.

Teach your children, "Whatever you do, whether in word or deed, do it all in the name of the Lord Jesus" (Col. 3:17).

Their Time

Explain that God will not force Himself on us. We must choose and plan to worship Him. We must set aside time for God.

His Blessings

Teach your kids that when they do what God has ordained them to do—when they praise Him—He will bless them immeasurably. They will discover His presence, His joy, His strength, His peace, and His guidance.

Our Call

It is our duty as children's leaders to help children enter the presence of God and glorify His name. As Dick Gruber has written: "You are a gatekeeper. Each Sunday Jesus gives you the opportunity to swing wide that gate and let the praise of children out" (*Children's Church: Turning Your Circus Into a Service*).

Show and Tell: Object Lessons

Shelia Stewart

How would you explain *sanctification* to a child? What about *eternity* or *omnipresence*? A child must understand what is being said before he or she can believe.

It is our responsibility as children's leaders to communicate spiritual truth in a way (language) that children can understand. An object lesson is an attempt to turn something that is difficult to understand into something children can touch, see, hear, taste, or smell.

Jesus, the Master Teacher, set the example for us by using common, everyday objects such as bread, flowers, birds, and coins to get important points across to His listeners. He used the familiar objects of life to clarify the unfamiliar truths of heaven.

If a picture is worth a thousand words, then an object—something with depth, texture, and dimension—must be priceless. Studies have shown that we remember much more of what we see and hear than of what we hear alone. Object lessons help explain abstract spiritual truths by concrete tangible means. Drawing a parallel between the known and unknown can make a vivid and lasting impression.

Types of Object Lessons

Object lessons can be grouped into four general categories:

Objects from nature: a limb, a fig, a nest, etc. These can illustrate a parable from nature or add life to a Bible story.

Everyday objects: a cup, a dollar bill, a telephone. Man-made items you can find around the house can help to illustrate spiritual truths.

Special objects: Chemistry experiments, gospel illusions, and chalk talks fall into this category.

Human object lessons: People are the objects! A pyramid of people can illustrate the sandy foundation Jesus warned about; a person's head of hair can remind us that Jesus has every hair numbered.

Eight Rules to Follow

1. Keep it brief—three or four minutes at most.
2. Use vocabulary children will understand. Don't talk over their heads.
3. Focus on one main point.
4. Make sure the prop is large enough to be seen and that everyone can see it.
5. Plan ahead and gather objects in advance.
6. Be thoroughly familiar with the content you are presenting.
7. Practice, practice, practice. Don't assume anything.
8. Depend on and allow the Lord to speak through you to the hearts of the children.

Age Appropriateness

Because young children think concretely, you can't expect them to "get" the message in a typical object lesson—a lesson where the object represents something other than itself. In the minds of preschoolers and early elementary kids, a cloud is a cloud, period.

But you can and should use objects in teaching young kids . . . if you steer away from symbolism. For example, you can point to a flock of birds (or a picture of a bird) in teaching the truth that God's eye is on the sparrow. Or you can use large nails in telling about the Crucifixion.

Symbolic object lessons are most effective with preteens, but can also be used with third- and fourth-graders.

Two Questions

Ruth Haycock says teachers should ask themselves two questions before using an object in a lesson: "First, does this object actually make the truth more clear, or are the relationships so symbolic that they make learning the real truth more difficult? Second, is the child so mystified by the object or action related to it that he remembers only the action and loses the meaning entirely?" (*Childhood Education in the Church*).

If an object helps a child understand sanctification or eternity or some other biblical truth, we should use it.

Sample Object Lessons

Our Heavenly Father Is Wise

Prop: One piece of a jigsaw puzzle and the puzzle box

Point: "For God . . . knows everything" (1 John 3:20).

Presentation: I've got a big challenge for someone. Who wants to volunteer?

(Hand a puzzle piece to a volunteer. Ask him to describe the whole picture using only his piece. When he cannot do it, show the picture on the box. Now he will probably be able to show you where his piece fits.)

Seeing the whole picture helps the little pieces make sense, doesn't it?

We see our life only one piece at a time, but God sees the whole picture—from beginning to end. He understands the things that make no sense to us.

Our Heavenly Father Is Loving

Props: A large relighting candle and a book of matches

Point: "I have loved you with an everlasting love" (Jer. 31:3).

Presentation: I'm going to light a candle, and I want us to pretend that the flame is God's love. (Light the candle.)

Do you think there is anything you could do that would cause God to stop loving you? (As each child offers a suggestion—such as lying, stealing, murder—have him blow out the candle. It will relight each time.)

Just as we cannot blow out this candle, we cannot end God's love for us. His love never stops.

Our Heavenly Father Is Always Present

Prop: Battery-operated radio

Point: "You are all around me—in front and in back" (Ps. 139:5 ICB).

Presentation: Look at the air around you. Do you see anything? Is anything there?

(Display the battery-operated radio). Radio waves are everywhere—all around us. We can't see them or feel them or hear them, but they're always there.

(Turn on the radio and locate a station).

We can't see God either, but He is everywhere. We will never be alone because He has promised to always be with us.

Our Heavenly Father Is Trustworthy

Prop: Blindfold

Point: "In you they trusted and were not disappointed" (Ps. 22:5).

Presentation: Who trusts me? (Select a volunteer and blindfold him. Stand him on a table or sturdy chair. Ask him to turn around and place his heels on the edge of the platform.)

(As you talk to him, move away from the child and have another adult stand directly behind him.) I won't let you get hurt. You'll be safe. Do you trust me?

(When he says yes, ask him to put his hands by his side and fall backwards. Obviously you won't sound close enough to catch him, so it may take lots of encouragement to get the child to follow through. When he does, complete the lesson.)

People and things sometimes disappoint us, but God will never let us down. If He said it, He'll do it. He can be completely trusted.

Our Heavenly Father Is Unchanging

Props: A bottle of bubbles and several pieces of heavy floral wire

Point: "I the Lord do not change" (Mal. 3:6).

Presentation: Let's see what interesting designs you can come up with by bending these wires into different shapes. (Hand out the wires to volunteers.) Can anyone make a square wire and then blow a square bubble? What about a flower shape? Or a triangle?

(Let the children experiment with the wires and the bubbles. No matter what the shape of the wire, the bubbles will always be round.)

No matter how the situations around us change, God remains the same.

Prepared for Service (by Debbie Mason)

Props: A shiny container such as a silver or stainless teapot, clear cup or glass, and water

Point: "In a large house there are things made out of gold and silver . . . the Master will be able to use them for honorable purposes. They will be made holy. They will be ready to do any good work" (2 Tim. 2:20-21 NIRV).

Presentation: Look at this container. Isn't it pretty? What is its purpose? If it is not being used, it is not doing what it was created to do.

Jesus wants to fill us with His Spirit so He can use us to minister to others. (Pour water into your container as you describe how God pours His Holy Spirit and gifts into one's life.)

Of course, it doesn't do much good to be filled unless what's inside is poured out and shared. (Place empty cup on the table.) This pitcher of water won't help a thirsty person unless the water is poured out of the pitcher.

Can this pitcher pour its water out alone—without any help? No, someone has to control it. (Explain how we should be controlled by Jesus. He will make us holy and prepare us to do good works.)

There are lots of spiritually thirsty people in the world. (Name some ways people may be spiritually thirsty.) Jesus can use us to help them.

If we are being used by Jesus, He will be able to see Himself in us. (Pass around the container and let the children see their reflection.) Do you want to be used in His service?

Our Personal Alarm (by Debbie Mason)

Props: Hand-held alarm (like the ones attached to a key chain)

Point: "I guide you in the way of wisdom and lead you along straight paths" (Prov. 4:11).

Presentation: God has sent the Holy Spirit to lead us and to help us avoid sin and danger. Suppose you were thinking about cheating on a test? (Set the alarm off.) The Holy Spirit would sound an inner alarm to let you know cheating is wrong. (Ask the children to name other situations where the Holy Spirit might correct us or protect us.)

Developing and Delivering Dynamic Children's Messages

Lance Colkmire

The preaching of the Word of God should be the most dynamic part of your weekly kids church service. Does that statement intimidate you? Your answer probably depends on how you define *dynamic*. This word does not mean "emotionally supercharged" (seeing kids cry is not necessarily an evidence that your sermon was "spiritual"). Nor does dynamic mean "hyped up" (you know, like a shaken-up can of Pepsi—lots of fizz and froth). Nor does it mean always-better-than last-week's message ("How can I top that Samson-bursting-his-chains escape trick?").

What Makes a Children's Sermon Dynamic?

Dynamic comes from the Greek word *dunamis*. In the Bible it is translated as "powerful," "able," and "mighty." A dynamic children's sermon is one which manifests God's power—it is God's ability in action. As a result, a mighty work is done.

His Power

First, a dynamic children's sermon displays God's power. Simon Peter preached that kind of message after he was filled with the Holy Spirit on the Day of Pentecost. The same man who had denied even knowing Jesus just a few weeks before now stood before a crowd of thousands and boldly declared, "God has made this Jesus, whom you crucified, both Lord and Christ" (Acts 2:36).

If the Holy Spirit could give Peter such boldness, surely He can do the same for you as you stand before your sometimes unruly "mob" on Sunday mornings!

Divine Ability in Action

Second, a dynamic sermon is really God's ability in action. As Peter preached, the listeners "were cut to the heart and said . . . 'What shall we do?'" (Acts 2:37). It was the convicting power of the Spirit—not Peter's great oratory—that cut them deeply.

For two nights straight, eight-year-old Jeremy did nothing but disrupt others as I ministered at a children's camp in Michigan. But something changed the third night. From beginning to end, he was captivated by the message on casting our burdens on the Lord. When I gave the altar call, Jeremy was the first to respond, and I had the honor of helping him pray about a heavy family burden he was carrying. The Holy Spirit had taken 1 Peter 5:7 and driven it into that troubled boy's heart.

Mighty Work

Third, a dynamic sermon does a mighty work. On the Day of Pentecost, "those who accepted his [Peter's] message were baptized, and about three thousand were added to their number that day" (Acts 2:41).

In kids church, the mighty work might be a girl accepting Christ, a boy trusting God for his grandfather's salvation, or a girl raising her hands in sincere worship for the first time. All those are works that the Word of God and the Holy Spirit can bring about.

The Word's Work

Since God works through His Word, the children's sermon must be Scripture-focused. This does not mean rattling off as many Bible verses as you can; rather, it means focusing on one particular Bible truth and hammering it home.

For the Word of God to be able to accomplish its mission, your preaching must meet three criteria:

1. It must be accurate. Don't deliver opinions or personal convictions, and never preach anything you'll have to "un-preach" later.
2. It must be clear. Put it on the kids' level. Answer the question "What does this scripture mean?"
3. It must be relevant. Answer the question, "What does this passage have to say to boys and girls?"

How to Prepare a Dynamic Children's Sermon

Here are the nominees for the five sorriest types of children's sermons I've ever witnessed (or preached myself!):

1. *Out of touch.* Some messages are too impersonal or too abstract to speak to kids.

2. *"Wind me up and let me go."* This is the kind of message I've seen from a couple of children's evangelists—the prepackaged, here-we go-again, I-don't-even-have-to-think-about-what-I'm-saying sermon.

3. *Straight from the hip.* Even kids can smell (almost literally!) when a sermon is a last-minute effort.

4. *Too high and too long.* When a message shoots over kids' heads or wears them out, expect them to start acting like children before it's over.

5. *"Gotta use this gadget."* The children's pastor has this neat new gadget—maybe a flaming Bible or a needle-through-the-balloon trick—and makes it the focus of his or her presentation.

Improper preparation is the foundational problem with each of these sermon types. Here's how to avoid those problems and build a dynamic sermon.

Get in Touch

Building friendships with kids—learning about their families, their needs, their interests, and their relationship with God—is the beginning point for being able to minister effectively to them. For example, if you discover that some kids are from broken homes, that's a subject you should address. If you learn that few of your kids have personal devotions, there's another potential sermon.

Not only will building relationships help you choose relevant topics, but it will also make kids receptive to you and the gospel you preach.

Get With God

Before you prepare a children's sermon, you should . . .

1. Evaluate yourself—make sure your own life measures up to your message.
2. Pray for God's direction and anointing.
3. Pray (and sometimes fast) for God to do a mighty work among the children.

Go for a Goal

Having a topic in mind is not enough; you must then narrow it down to a specific, realistic aim. For instance:

- In response to this message on worship, the kids will praise God by kneeling and telling God why they love Him.

- After this salvation message, kids will be given the opportunity to ask God to forgive them of their sins and become the boss of their life.

Get on Their Level

Once your subject and goal are established, you must construct a message that is on the kids' level. Your basic framework should look like this:

1. Introduce the topic, showing your kids that today's message will relate to them.
2. Declare what God's Word says about this topic.
3. Show kids how to apply God's Word to their situation.
4. Challenge them to respond.

Gather Your Tools

Plan to make your children's sermon as visual as possible. If you see that using a flaming Bible or a needle-through-the-balloon trick will help convey your message, then use it! Just don't let the tail wag the dog.

Delivering a Dynamic Children's Sermon

No matter how hard you prepare, nothing significant will happen if you fail to effectively communicate your message. Preaching to kids requires arresting their attention, feeding them the Word, and calling for a specific response.

Grab Their Attention

"Sit up straight and listen, boys and girls. Today's message is from the Book of Isaiah. It's about a king named Uzziah."

Boring! That is not the way to begin a children's message. Instead, a dynamic sermon will grab the children's attention by speaking to them where they are. For instance, a message on fear might begin with the question, "What are you afraid of?" A message on worship might begin, "If Jesus walked into kids church, what would He say about the way you have worshiped Him today?"

Feed Them

Once you have established the subject and have the kids' attention, it is time to feed them the Word of God. Here are four guidelines:

1. Don't preach a principle without concrete examples. Simply teaching "Cast your burden on the Lord" is not enough—it's too abstract. You must talk about specific burdens—the death of a loved one, a broken home, a financial need—for kids to get it.

2. Put purpose in your storytelling. Don't tell a Bible story simply because stories captivate kids; instead, use a story to convey a focused message. For instance, what single point could you convey in telling about David and Goliath? the crossing of the Red Sea? the resurrection of Lazarus?

3. Stimulate the children's senses. Smell, sight, taste, touch—the more your message involves these four senses, the more children will remember it. So when you tell the story of Mary washing Jesus' feet, let the kids sniff perfume. When you tell about the feeding of the 5,000, let kids eat goldfish crackers. When preaching about the Crucifixion, bring sharp thorns for the kids to touch and large nails for the kids to see.

4. Maximize your words. When you're speaking, don't talk in a monotone. Speak quickly . . . then slowly . . . then loudly . . . then softly—adjusting your sentences to fit the mood. And use simple terminology the kids can understand.

Call for a Response

At the end of your message, challenge the kids to make a specific response. For instance: "Come forward if you want to pray for the salvation of someone you love" or "Kneel at your seat and praise the Lord for three ways He is blessing you."

I'll never forget the night in Texas when I preached a children's sermon on worship. I emphasized that the object of our worship is that on which we spend our time, our money, our thoughts, and our energies. My focus was that Jesus wants to be the Lord of our life—the one we genuinely worship.

During the altar time, I prayed with an eight-year-old boy who was quietly weeping. When I asked him what he was praying about, he said, "I've been worshiping my baseball cards."

My simple message had triggered a life-changing response in that little boy! That night he asked Jesus to become the most important love of His life.

What Do I Preach About?

Sanctification . . . the Second Coming . . . healing . . . deliverance . . . just about any doctrine that can be preached to adults can be preached to kids. The challenge, of course, is communicating on their level.

Look at it like this: Do the kids to whom you minister need salvation, healing, deliverance, or sanctification? Then preach about it! Do they need to pray, worship, witness, or give offerings? Then preach it!

Sample Sermon: "Examine Yourselves"

On one side of a poster board, write the first two words of 1 Corinthians 13:5 (Examine yourselves . . .). On the other side, write the last portion of the verse (Christ Jesus is in you; unless, of course, you fail the test).

Bring an eye-exam chart with you or make your own. Also bring items used in a physical exam (such as a tongue depressor, a thermometer, and a stethoscope.) Display only the "Christ Jesus . . . " part of the verse as you begin.

How many of you like to take tests? According to 2 Corinthians 13:5, there is a test you can take that shows whether or not Jesus Christ is living in you. *Have the kids read this portion of the verse with you.* What kind of test do you think this verse is talking about? Let's try to find out. I will need several volunteers to help me with some experiments.

First, I want to give three people a spelling test. *Choose kids who say they are good spellers. Have one write the words* church, Jesus, *and* Bible *on a marker board. Another should write* love, prayer, *and* worship. Witness, obey, *and* joy *should be spelled by the third volunteer.*

Good work! Each of you passes the spelling test. But does this test prove if Jesus is living in you? No. Let's try another.

Have a child come forward and stand on one side of the room while you display the eye chart on the opposite side. Have her cover one eye and try to read the letters on the various lines. Then have her cover the other eye and try again.

Well, your vision is fine. But I'm afraid that doesn't show us whether or not Jesus is living in you.

Now call two kids forward and give them a strength test by having them arm-wrestle. Then say to the winner, I'm glad I didn't try to arm-wrestle with you! But physical strength doesn't tell us whether or not you pass the Christ-is-in-you test.

Call someone else forward and use whatever medical tools you came up with to diagnose their health. You appear to be healthy, but these instruments can't show me whether or not Jesus is living within you. In fact, even if I had an X-ray machine, it would not show us if you pass the test.

We have tried several tests, and everyone tested has done pretty well. But we still haven't found a test that can show whether or not Jesus is part of someone's life. And the Bible says there is one.

OK, I have to confess—I've been keeping something from you. I haven't shown you the first two words of 2 Corinthians 13:5. *Reveal the words "Examine yourselves."*

You have to test yourself! Only you and Jesus can know for certain if He is living within you.

We test ourselves not by spelling words or arm-wrestling or using a thermometer. Instead, the tool we use is God's Word. Ask yourselves three questions:

1. Have I asked Jesus to forgive me of my sins? First John 1:9 says, "If we confess our sins, he is faithful and just and will forgive us our sins."

    Write the word Forgiven *on the marker board.*

2. Am I following Jesus' commandments? Jesus said, "If you love Me, you will obey what I command" (John 14:15).

    Write the words Following His Commands *on the board.*

3. Am I growing good fruit in my life? Ephesians 5:9 says, "For the fruit of the light consists in all goodness."

   Write Good Fruit *on the board.*

   In this test, three F's—*forgiven, following,* and *fruit*—equal an A! When you ask Jesus to forgive you of your sins, He comes into your life. Then He gives you both the desire and the strength to begin following His commandments. As He lives in you, He grows good fruit in your life—things like love, peace, and patience.

   Is Jesus living in you? Do you pass the test?

   Ask the boys and girls to bow their heads and quietly examine themselves. Then lead into a time of prayers in which they can receive Christ.

Altering Kids' Lives at the Altar

Lance Colkmire

I was saved at a church altar when I was 10 years old. . . . At age 12, I was baptized in the Holy Spirit at a church altar. . . . As a teenager, the Lord often gave me guidance, peace and strength as I knelt at an altar. . . . As a young adult, the Lord confirmed whom my wife would be as I prayed at an altar.

Just as the church altar has had an awesome impact on my life, so I believe that today God wants to alter kids' lives at the altar.

The Altar in Scripture

Since the time of Noah, the altar has been central to God's plan.

A Place to Meet with God

When the first wave of tens of thousands of Hebrews returned from 70 years of exile, the first part of God's house they rebuilt was the altar. Once built, "they offered burnt offerings on it to the Lord" (Ezra 3:3 NKJV). They wanted God to be with them, so they "built the altar . . . to offer burnt offerings . . . as it is written in the Law of Moses" (v. 2 NKJV).

In many churches today, we need to "rebuild" the altar. The altar service has traditionally been a focal part of the Pentecostal worship service, but in too many churches the altar no longer receives the attention it deserves.

Let's change this! Because our children need to meet with God, and because the altar is one place where this should be happening, let's do all we can to emphasize ministry at the altar

A Place of Remembrance

When the Lord appeared to Abraham at Shechem, promising him, "To your descendants I will give this land," Abraham responded by building an altar to the Lord (Gen. 12:7 NKJV).

When the angel of the Lord appeared to Gideon, the farmer feared for his life. But the Lord spoke peace to him. "So Gideon built an altar to the Lord there and called it The Lord is Peace" (Judg. 6:24).

For both Abraham and Gideon, the altars they built were altars of remembrance. These were monuments of rock they could point to and say, "The Lord spoke to me here."

Our children need such monuments! How wonderful for a child to be able to point to an altar and say, "I remember when God answered my prayer as I cried out to Him there."

A Place of Cleansing

When Isaiah saw a vision of the Lord in the temple, he cried, "I am ruined! For I am a man of unclean lips . . . and my eyes have seen the King, the Lord Almighty" (Isa. 6:5). But then an angel removed a hot coal from the altar and touched Isaiah's lips with it. And the angel said, "Your guilt is taken away and your sin atoned for" (v. 7).

Wow! There is nothing more exciting than seeing an unsaved child have his guilt taken away as he or she kneels before God at an altar. It is our job as children's pastors and teachers to regularly give children the chance to receive Christ at a church altar.

A Place of Healing

Jesus said that if you approach an altar and then remember that someone has something against you, you must "first go and be reconciled to your brother; then come and offer your gift" (Matt. 5:23-24).

In our day, countless children have lives filled with fractured family relationships. They need to know that Jesus is not only concerned about their relationship with Him, but also about their relationships with others. In fact, the two go hand-in-hand. He wants to help them to forgive and to receive the forgiveness of others.

A Place of Intercession

When God sent a terrible plague upon Israel because of their rebellion against Him, "David built an altar to the Lord . . . and sacrificed burnt offerings and fellowship offerings. Then the Lord answered prayer in behalf of the land, and the plague on Israel was stopped" (2 Sam. 24:25).

Today, God will use children in the ministry of intercession if we will so train them at our church altars. He will use them to help bring about revival.

A Place of Thanksgiving and Praise

When Noah's feet hit dry land after endless months on the ark, the first thing he did was build "an altar to the Lord" and offer "burnt offerings on it" (Gen. 8:20).

When Solomon dedicated the Temple to the Lord, the glory of the Lord filled the place. When the people "saw the fire coming down and the glory of the Lord above the temple, they knelt on the pavement with their faces to the ground, and they worshiped and gave thanks to the Lord" (2 Chron. 7:3).

As we minister to children, let's teach them how to worship the Lord at the altar, and let's provide opportunities for them to do so. Let's linger with them until the glory of the Lord fills the place! Let's show them the necessity of developing a lifestyle of praise and thanksgiving.

A Place to Sacrifice

In obedience to the Lord's command, Abraham placed the love of his life—his son Isaac—on an altar to sacrifice him to the Lord (Gen. 22:1-14). That's the spirit of total commitment described in Romans 12:1: "Offer your bodies as living sacrifices, holy and pleasing to God." That's the kind of commitment that can begin and develop at a church altar.

A Place to Learn

Maybe you've never thought of the altar as a teaching tool, but it should be. As the Israelites prepared to enter the Promised Land, Moses told them, "When you have crossed the Jordan into the land the Lord your God is giving you, set up some large stones. . . . Build there an altar to the Lord your God, an altar of stones. . . . And you shall write very clearly all the words of this law on these stones you have set up" (Deut. 27:2, 5, 8).

Every time the Israelites would see this stone "billboard," it would remind them of who had brought them into Canaan and how they were to live. This altar would be an ongoing teaching visual.

In our day, the altar should still be a place of instruction. This doesn't mean we have to engrave the laws of God on our altars (though that might not be a bad idea!) It does mean that when a child seriously responds to an altar call, we have one of those wonderful "teachable moments" in our hands. It is a time to talk with the child . . . to give him or her instruction from the Word of God . . . and to pray with him or her. The altar should be a place where children learn lessons they will never forget.

Nine Mistakes to Avoid

Whenever I teach a workshop on altar ministry, I always ask the participants, "Have you ever had a negative experience at a church altar that has made a lasting impression on you?" There is always at least one person who raises his or her hand and then gives a sad testimony. Usually, the bad experience was caused by the unwise action of an altar worker.

Yes, there are sincere Christians who hinder children instead of helping them when they come forward to pray. Let's look at nine common mistakes we must avoid.

Assuming Why the Child Responded

No matter how specific the altar call, kids often respond for a different reason. For instance, it is a giant mistake to assume that all the kids who respond to an invitation to receive Christ are coming forward for salvation. Thus it is crucial to always ask the responding child, "Why did you come to the altar?" Following the child's response, the altar worker will be able to pray intelligently with the child.

Not Taking a Child's Request

"My pet lizard's tail broke off."

"I don't like my new glasses."

"I'm afraid of what's under my bed and in my closet."

Requests like those might seem unimportant to us, but not to the child . . . and not to God. First Peter 5:7 says, "Give all your worries to Him, for He cares for you" (CEV). If children learn how to give their simplest needs to God today, they will likely turn their complex needs over to Him in the years to come.

If something is important enough to bring a child to the altar, it is important enough for us to help him pray about.

Using Religious Jargon

As we talk with kids at the altar, we must use simple and specific language. This means avoiding terms such as "born again," "saved," and" sanctified." For instance, instead of asking, "Are you saved?" you could ask, "Have you ever asked Jesus to take away your sins?"

Agreeing with a Misdirected Request

Ten-year-old Brian wanted me to help him pray that his parents would get back together. But his parents had divorced many years earlier, and each now had a different spouse. That was a misdirected request, asking that two more divorces take place so a remarriage could occur.

I told Brian why it would be wrong for us to pray that way. Instead, we asked God to give Brian the peace he needed to live with his situation. As we prayed, God did just that! Brian's countenance totally changed as he began praying in the Spirit.

The point is this—we must help children pray in agreement with God's Word.

Not Letting the Child Pray

As important as it is for us to pray for children at the altar, it is even more important that we help the children themselves to pray.

Some kids don't know how to pray; others will be content with letting us pray for them while they just kneel there. It is our responsibility to encourage children to pray by offering them simple instructions and then praying with them.

As a child prays, I like to agree with her in prayer, whispering my prayer in her ear. For instance: "Jesus, thank You for hearing Mandy as she asks You to help her stop lying. I know You love Mandy and want to help her obey You."

Rebuking a Child

I'll never forget one lonesome boy who lingered at an altar for a very long time. In talking with him, I discovered he wasn't technically praying about anything. Instead, he was simply soaking in the love of peers and adults who were laying their hands on him and calling his name in prayer.

I could have sent the boy back to his seat, but I didn't. The positive experience he was having—even if he wasn't seeking God with words—would stay with him. His idea of God and prayer, as shaped by those who prayed for him that day, would draw him toward the Father and the church.

Expecting a Certain Response

Some adults will question or even discredit a child's spiritual experience if he or she doesn't respond in an adultlike manner. (*If a child doesn't cry or doesn't stay at the altar a long time, how can they experience be genuine?* they wonder.)

What they forget is that Jesus never told children to become like adults in their manner of approaching Him. Instead, Jesus told His disciples they had to become like kids to inherit the kingdom of heaven.

As we pray with children, let's not question their exemplary faith and humility that enable them to take God at His word.

Letting a Child Get Out of Control

I've seen many children's workers fail to use discernment when a child became overly emotional during an altar service. Outward actions such as crying, shouting, and lying prostrate are sometimes products of the Spirit's working, and we never want to hinder that. At other times, however, such expressions are simply the child getting himself "hyped up," and we want to discourage that.

How can we tell the difference? First, we should pray for discernment. Second, we must quickly answer these question: Are the child's actions

- bringing glory to God or simply drawing attention to the child?
- helping or hindering the prayers of others?

- in keeping with the Spirit's working in that service?
- helping the child himself draw closer to God?

If you discern that a child needs direction, you should go to the child, help him calm down by quietly talking with him, have the child tell you about God's goodness to him, perhaps say a sentence prayer with him, then help him return to his seat.

Remember, the point is not to question the child's sincerity. It's just that the child can be sincerely wrong! By intervening where necessary, you will not quench the Spirit. Instead, you will help the child, the other children, and the altar service.

Failing to Follow Up

After I prayed with Kenny at a youth camp altar in Florida, I asked him, "Do you believe the Lord has forgiven your sins?"

"No," was his blunt answer.

"Why not?"

Kenny replied, "Because I don't feel anything."

I opened my Bible and read Ephesians 2:8-9. Then I explained that salvation comes through faith, not feelings.

I asked Kenny if he wanted to pray again—for assurance. He did.

After we prayed, Kenny explained, "I feel it! I feel it!"

As camp wound down the next day, Kenny peppered me with questions about Christian living. But what would have happened if I had not followed up on his initial prayer?

Make it a practice to talk with the children you pray for after they say "Amen." Inform parents about a child's spiritual decision. And follow up with the child directly in the subsequent days and weeks.

The Altar Call

Of course, you cannot minister to children at the altar if they don't come! So here are six steps in giving an altar call to children.

1. Prepare yourself.

   As a minister to children, it is your job to pray, fast, and get in tune with God's heart in preparation for delivering the gospel. Before you preach a message, you must measure yourself by it. If you're not living up to it, your kids will know . . . sooner or later.

2. Prepare their hearts.

   The better your relationship with the children, the better they will hear your message. And the more you intercede on their behalf, the more they will respond.

   In the service itself, everything should build to the time of response. When that time arrives, worshipful music will help them focus their attention.

3. Be specific.

   At the conclusion of your message, make your appeal specific. For instance:

   - If you've never asked Jesus to take away your sins . . . .
   - If you want to pray for an unsaved friend . . . .
   - If you need God's help to enable you break a sin habit . . . .

4. Motivate with the Word.

   As you ask children to come forward, motivate them with the Word of God, which is the source of genuine faith. For instance:

- The Bible says, "The blood of Jesus Christ . . . cleanses us from all sin" (1 John 1:7 NKJV). Will you come forward and ask Him to forgive you today?

- The Bible says God wants all people to "come to repentance" (2 Peter 3:9). Will you come forward and pray for someone you know who needs Jesus?

- The Bible says we can do "all things through Christ" (Phil. 4:13). Will you come forward and ask Jesus to help you break a sin habit?

5. Pray with kids as a group.

   Before letting the kids pray individually, I usually pray with them as a group. Sometimes I do this while they're at their seat; at other times I do this after they come forward. Either way, I lead them in a simple model prayer which they repeat after me. This helps to prepare them for their personal prayers.

6. Rely on the Holy Spirit.

   I have seen children saved . . . filled with the Spirit . . . called into ministry . . . healed . . . and delivered at church altars. In every case, it was the Holy Spirit who did the work.

If we want to see children's lives altered at the altar, we must rely fully on Him.

Reflect and Respond

1. *Help! Where Do I Begin?*

   A. Hebrews 4:15 says, "For we do not have a high priest who is unable to sympathize with our weaknesses." How do you suppose Jesus coming to earth as a baby and growing through the various stages of childhood enables Him to "sympathize" with the needs of children?

   B. Read three passages about Jesus ministering to children and their parents in desperate situations: Matthew 17:14-18; Mark 5:40-43, and Luke 7:11-17. What insights can you gain about being more responsive to the requests of parents?

   C. Jesus touched and blessed children. Do you make a weekly effort to give children appropriate physical touch? Side hugs, pats on the back, high fives, and handshakes communicate acceptance to children. Also, do you sometimes bless children by touching their forehead and praying God's favor on them?

2. *Children in the Church: Covenant Participants*

   A. Read 2 Timothy 1:3-7. Describe how both Timothy's family and his mentor, Paul, influenced his spiritual life. What does this example reveal about effective ministry to young people?

   B. How should the community of believers view children (Ps. 127:3)?

   C. What does Deuteronomy 6:4-9 reveal about how children are to come to know God?

   D. According to 2 Corinthians 3:3, how can children best discover what it means to follow Christ?

E. Describe a specific step your church should take now to embrace children as part of the life of the congregation.

3. Life-Changing Children's Leaders

A. According to James 3:1 and Matthew 18:6, how serious is the responsibility of teaching and leading kids?

B. Explain what it means to have a burden for ministry and why it is necessary.

C. In your role as a children's leader, rate yourself (from 1 to 5 stars) in each of these areas:
- An advocate for children
- A shepherd of children
- An administrator of children's programming
- An evangelist to children
- A worship leader for children

How can you strengthen your two weakest areas?

D. How can you encourage your church's teachers to "pastor" their classes?

4. Building a Team

A. Why is a leader's vision for children's ministry a critical factor in attracting and keeping volunteers?

B. What is your church's vision for ministry to children?

C. How are Jesus' words in Matthew 9:37-38 both an encouragement and an ongoing strategy in building a ministry team?

D. Why is a personalized invitation to get involved in children's ministry more effective than an announcement to the entire church?

Reflect and Respond

E. As a leader, list two specific steps you need take to foster a stronger team approach in your children's ministry.

5. Financing Ministry to Children

A. How is your church's ministry to children funded?

B. Why is it important to teach children to be givers, and how can you more effectively do this?

C. Describe an idea from the "Seek, Knock, and Ask" section that could help you obtain materials for your ministry to children.

6. Reaching the "In Between" Preteens

A. What is the greatest challenge in ministering to preteens?

B. What makes ministering to this age group so rewarding?

C. Describe an idea from this chapter that can improve your church's ministry to preteens.

7. Losing Teeth and Finding God

A. Why does the writer present such a wide variety of teaching methods for kids ages six to nine?

B. What does the writer say is the most valuable lesson we can teach this age group? Do you agree or disagree, and why?

C. Most early graders are cooperative with adults, and want to excel and please. How can you maximize those traits in ministering to this group?

8. Loving and Leading Preschoolers

A. "Teachers of young children must develop methods of working with their energy instead of against it," the writer says. List a couple of ways to do this.

B. Look at the "What to Teach" section of the chapter. How can you ensure that children at your church are taught those truths during their preschool years?

C. Why is it easy for preschoolers to have great faith in God, and how can we nurture that faith?

D. Describe ways preschoolers can minister to adults.

9. Burps, Diapers, and Joy: Baby Ministry

A. Why is effective care for newborns so critical?

B. List one way your church can improve its care for young parents (and parents-to-be).

C. What makes for an effective baby dedication?

D. How can a church nursery move past babysitting into ministry?

10. Building a Lesson Kids Will Love

A. How much time does it take to prepare an effective lesson for children?

B. Explain the statement, "Kids will be active on their terms or they will be active on your terms."

Reflect and Respond

C. Describe the type of testing we can give children in response to our Bible lessons.

D. List the three-step strategy that can work for every Bible lesson.

11. Scripture Memory: It Can Be Done

A. Why is it important for children to memorize Bible verses?

B. List three Bible verses you think are critical for children to memorize, and explain why.

C. What new method from this chapter do you believe can work for you?

D. Write out an important Scripture verse you learned during your childhood or teen years.

12. Disciplining the Undisciplined Child

A. How can building relationships improve children's behavior?

B. When you teach children, what are your expectations regarding their behavior?

C. How do you communicate your expectations for their behavior?

D. Why are some children's leaders such poor disciplinarians, and how can they change?

13. Welcoming the New Kid

A. Do you think parents perceive your church as a safe place for their kids? Why or why not?

B. What step should you take immediately to make your church more kid-friendly?

C. If children are not leaving your church with smiles on their faces, how can you change that?

14. Leading Children to Christ

A. Why does it mean to "pre-evangelize" young children, and why is this important?

B. When is a boy or girl ready to receive Christ as Savior?

C. List three mistakes a leader could make in child evangelism.

D. How can this chapter help you lead children to Christ more effectively?

15. Reaching Unchurched Kids

A. How can you help kids from non-Christian homes feel part of your church family?

B. Why is it important to help meet basic physical needs of unchurched kids?

C. Respond to the key point in the "Assign Them" section. Why is this critical?

D. How is Galatians 6:9 relevant in outreach ministry?

E. In "When Unchurched Children Come to Church," what does the writer mean by "Communicate Clearly"? How can you do this more effectively?

Reflect and Respond

16. Helping Kids Develop a Devotional Life

A. Describe a new step you can take to encourage kids to use their Bibles at church.

B. Describe a new step you can take in helping children to pray.

C. What can you do to help children practice personal devotions?

17. Reaching Out to Grieving Children

A. Next to each crisis listed below, list the initials of children in your church who have experienced it:
- Separation or divorce of parents
- Child suffering serious illness
- Neglect or abuse
- Death of a close relative
- Financial emergency
- Natural disaster (fire, flood, tornado, etc.)

B. How can you and your church improve the way you respond to grieving children?

18. Baptism, Communion, and Footwashing

A. What does water baptism represent?

B. What steps should you take to prepare children for water baptism?

C. Describe the spiritual blessings of participation in the Lord's Supper.

D. Why should we involve children in the sacrament of footwashing?

19. Children Can Pray, Walk, and Live in the Spirit

A. How should Acts 2:38-39 serve as a guidepost in your ministry to children?

B. List three ways the Holy Spirit can help children whom you serve.

C. What should you teach children about speaking in tongues?

D. How can you provide opportunities for children to receive the baptism in the Holy Spirit?

20. Helping Kids Find, Develop, and Use Their Gifts

A. Why is it important to help children discover their gifts?

B. List some of the gifts and talents God has given the children you serve.

C. How can you provide more opportunities for kids to use their gifts?

21. Expecting God to Show Up in Our Children's Worship Service

A. How is *planning* a significant part of a service in which the Holy Spirit moves?

B. How can we help children activate their faith in kids church?

C. What is the most valuable insight you gain from this chapter?

22. Let the Children Praise Him!

A. Based on Psalm 8:2 and Matthew 21:16, describe the power of children in worship.

B. List three ways you can inspire children to worship God.

C. In response to this chapter, describe one new way you will encourage children to worship God.

23. Show and Tell: Object Lessons

A. Write a simple object on faith using an object from nature.

B. Write a simple object lesson on giving using an everyday object.

24. Developing and Delivering Dynamic Children's Messages

A. What makes a children's sermon dynamic?

B. How can you ensure that your message is biblically accurate, on the kids' level, and relevant to their lives?

C. Why is it important to have a specific goal in mind when preparing a children's message?

D. Describe three mistakes a person could make in delivering a children's message.

25. Altering Kids' Lives at the Altar

A. Describe a significant spiritual experience you have had at a church altar.

B. Of the "Nine Mistakes to Avoid," which three do you think are the most common?

C. When presenting an altar call, what does it mean to motivate children with the Word of God? Why is this important?

D. How can a leader partner with the Holy Spirit in altar ministry?

Children's Ministry Certification Program

The purpose of the certification program is threefold:
1. Help to build a network of trained and specialized children's ministry leaders.
2. Enhance the status and credibility of children's ministry and the Children's Leaders Association within the Church of God.
3. Provide the basics in children's ministry training for local church volunteers as well as an entry point into full-time children's ministry.

Basics in Children's Ministry Certification
1. Read the entire *Reaching, Teaching, and Pastoring Children* manual.
2. Answer the "Reflect and Respond" questions for these chapters: 1, 2, 6-10.
3. Complete the application form in the back of this book.
4. Mail the application form and your answers to the "Reflect and Respond" questions.

Advanced Training Certification
1. Earn the "Basics in Children's Ministry" certificate.
2. Answer the "Reflect and Respond" questions for these chapters: 3-5, 11-25.
3. Read the three books on the certification list.
4. Complete the practicum.
5. Complete the application form in the back of this book.
6. Mail the application form and your answers to the "Reflect and Respond" questions.